How to Stop Overthinking for Good

The No B.S. Solution to Worry Less, Beat Procrastination, and Reclaim Your Time in Only 10 Minutes a Day

Shelomo Solson

Contents

Your Free Gift

As a thank you for your support, I'm offering you a free 40+ page digital workbook titled **How to Stop Overthinking Workbook**. It's a powerful resource designed to help you take action, gain clarity, and build better habits.

To access the workbook, visit:

www.LabelsToLegacy.com/Overthinking

Shelomo Solson

HOW TO STOP OVERTHINKING WORKBOOK

1

Inside, you'll find:

- Exercises to help you recognize thought patterns, emotional triggers, and mental roadblocks

- Simple tools to build positive habits through mindset work, daily trackers, and small daily shifts

- Goal-setting pages, habit bingo, and reflection prompts to help you take consistent action

This workbook is a great next step if you're ready to stop overthinking and start making meaningful progress.

Introduction

You may not control all the events that happen to you, but you can decide not to be reduced by them.

–Maya Angelou

Have you ever been trapped in an endless loop of "what-ifs"? You know, those questions that keep you going over the same problem or hypothetical situations. Those questions that make you think of every possible scenario without ever getting to a point.

What if I make the wrong choice? What if I fail? What if I lose my job? What if they don't like me? What if I'm not happy? What if I say the wrong thing? What if I don't have enough money? What if I get a terminal illness?

I can go on and on with examples of "what-if" questions that have filled my mind, but I'm sure you get the idea. In these moments of endless rumination and thinking up some of the most unlikely possibilities, every option seems like a risk. The fear of making the wrong move or not doing life perfectly becomes all-consuming.

The result? Paralysis. The complete inability to do anything other than think.

You're stuck, unable to decide or act, while time slips away. What's worse, every moment spent in this paralysis feels like a waste, a failure in itself. Yet, you can't seem to break free from this. You can't stop this cycle of anxiety. It's as if the more you think about a decision, the harder it becomes to make one.

So, what do you do? You wait. You hesitate. You second-guess yourself even more. And you don't do anything to change it.

I've been there. For far too long, I was trapped in a cycle of overthinking. I wanted to have complete control over my life. I wanted perfection. To make things even worse, I grew up as a people-pleaser, always chasing approval, measuring my worth by others' standards, seeking validation.

I think you know exactly what I mean, right? You see, you and I are similar. We both live in a world where we feel like any decision we make, whether it's about our careers, our fitness, our finances, or even our relationships, is put under a spotlight.

We live in a world where we often don't deal with our past traumas. We should be strong, and just the thought of showing others that we are hurt or have feelings fills our minds with even more uncertainties.

We live in a world where we feel like we should automatically have all the answers. And when we don't, we drain ourselves mentally thinking about everything we could've done better or differently.

We carry it with us daily, and at some point, it stops feeling like a passing thought. It becomes part of who we are. It takes over our entire being. No one warned us how fast that feeling could take over.

Like I said, I've been there. I've failed, too, and I mean *hard*.

I've lost relationships. I've been broke. I've fought anxiety—and I still do.

I have felt the pressure in my chest, the cold sweat on the back of my neck, and that feeling of weakness that only anxiety can give. Like you, I fight these small and big battles daily, and every day, I count victories and defeats.

Along the way, I learned my coping techniques, and I assure you that you will, too. There is a way out. That's why I'm writing this book.

For a long time, I didn't seek the help I needed. Perhaps I was too proud to admit I had a problem. Maybe I was scared of losing control. Perhaps I'm overthinking the endless possibilities for not seeking help for my overthinking soon enough.

Whatever the case was for me, I got out of that trap. Now, I want to help you.

I want my words to serve as tools—practical, real, and effective—for when you face your own struggles. My goal is for you to use the strategies and insights in this book to finally break free from overthinking and anxiety. My hope is for you to come out stronger on the other side.

Let me be brutally honest about something: There's no B.S. here.

I'm not going to tell you to stop thinking. You are not a robot. I'm not going to tell you that you should cut worry completely out of your life. It's just not possible. I'm also not going to bore you with fluff about blocking your feelings. You're human. You're allowed to have emotions, whether you want to show them or not.

What I am going to do is help you acknowledge that changing a habit like overthinking is hard. It can be very uncomfortable. But trust me, it will be worth it. And, while you can't stop thinking and worrying, you can limit them and stop overthinking for good.

I'm not a psychiatrist or psychologist. I have no formal medical or psychological training. What I do have is years of experience with overthinking and procrastination. I have done extensive research on finding strategies to help me stop these habits, which I'm going to share with you.

This book uses a clear and straightforward approach to help you challenge how you think, process uncertainties, and deal with analysis paralysis. More than once, it'll push you to your limit. But you can work through it.

You can start reclaiming your life. You can (and will) boss your fears because you'll learn how to identify the triggers of your overthinking and anxiety. You will recognize these moments for what they are. Applying the techniques we discuss in this book gives you the courage and tools to control them.

This isn't just another "change your mindset" book you'll forget the moment you're done reading it. In this book, you'll learn about practical exercises and activities to implement everything in your life.

We'll discuss how much you should let your repeating thoughts into your life. You can't block every thought you have. Some deserve a few minutes of your time. No more, no less. Determining how much each one needs is key.

The big bonus is that implementing the lessons in this book won't take over your life. Don't even start to overthink the amount of time you'll have to spend on it. It will be short lessons, only 10 minutes a day. But these few minutes will help to reprogram your mind and heart for better physical and mental health.

You also won't have to wait until the end of the book to start seeing a difference in your life. After laying the foundation of overthinking and its impact on your life in Chapter 1, we'll start with these short exercises at the end of every chapter.

Since the exercises are all chapter-specific, it will also be easy to revisit some of them if you struggle with certain aspects. You won't have to overthink which exercises you might have to redo. You'll know.

By the end of this book, you'll have a proven system to stop overthinking, make faster decisions, and free yourself from mental exhaustion. But remember, commitment is key.

Think of this as a new fitness routine. If you want bigger biceps and pecs, you have to do exercises that work those specific muscle groups to get physically stronger. The only difference is that the exercises in this book will improve your mental strength. Over time, you will become resilient to your rumination.

Remember, it's not the challenges that hold you back; it's the stories you keep telling yourself. The longer you let overthinking rule your life, the more time you waste. Now is the time to break free for good...

PART 1

Understanding How and Why Overthinking Is Holding You Back

CHAPTER 1

The Hidden Cost of Overthinking— And Why You Can't Ignore It Anymore

To think too much is a disease.

–Fyodor Dostoyevsky

Am I ever going to make it in life?

This is probably the question that has caused me the most anxiety and overthinking. It's the question I have lost the most sleep over. I have gone years working my butt off on the wrong things to chase this concept of "making it."

After things didn't work out exactly how I wanted, I beat myself up. Over and over again. Then, it became a cycle. I worked on trends instead of following my intuition. I developed insecurities in my life because I hadn't achieved my 10-year plan in a few months.

I continuously thought to myself, *I am not good enough*, even though people in my life were praising me for what I was able to achieve in a short amount of time.

Those insecurities became self-sabotage. I would sabotage my goals. I would sabotage my intimate relationships because I thought I wasn't good enough. I would sabotage my inner peace and not stay in the present.

I started creating made-up scenarios, like believing people were judging me or laughing because of my goals or what I posted on social media. Even if that was true at times, my mind would completely overexaggerate it.

I kept thinking my partner wasn't supportive of my career path. I constantly believed my partner saw me as a failure. I would even resent people around me who didn't have similar goals.

That made me question even more if I was ever going to make it. Not only was I harsh on myself, but I also continuously measured myself by the standards of others and what they thought of me.

In the hopes of getting their approval, I would select new goals that aligned with theirs, but I chased them without passion and drive. I held onto the weight of even the slightest failures. I didn't allow myself to manifest my next goal because I completely blocked off any manifestation of success.

You see, I have always tried to prove myself. At school, I was a straight-A student, but still, I believed I wasn't good enough. I got my first job at 16 to pay my own bills and was in leadership roles in my extracurricular activities. I won numerous competitions, from speech competitions to company pitches, and even the National Alumnus of the Year award for my entire fraternity.

Yet, I felt I wasn't good enough. The fear of not making it continued to weigh me down. I pushed myself beyond breaking point.

Eventually, I had a failing business. I was broken. I resorted to odd jobs to make ends meet: substitute teaching and driving for Uber. I was completely broke and had multiple anxiety attacks.

I knew I had to change. I realized I was focusing too much on the future. By overthinking, I wasn't only ruining my present but also sabotaging my future. I believe that moment was the turning point in my life.

I still have big goals, and I still work hard to achieve them, but I learned to trust the process. Instead of wondering, *Am I ever going to make it?* I realized that I needed to find myself again. I needed to work out what success means to me, not to other people. I had to dig deep and truly ask myself, *What do I really want in life?*

For me, this process started with truly understanding what overthinking is, how I was overthinking, and the impact it had on my life, not just my mental health but my physical body as well.

Understanding how your overthinking affects your life will help you to also identify the fears that cause your mind to spiral. Do you know what the best thing is about fear? It goes away as soon as we understand it and accept it in our lives.

What Is Overthinking?

Before we get into why we overthink and the effects it can have on our lives, let's first look at what overthinking is. You probably already know that it's thinking about a topic or situation so much that it takes over your life. You might be beating yourself up over a past mistake, stress about what's happening now, or be anxious about your future.

But how does it look in real life?

Say you have to do a presentation at work. You've spent hours preparing the information. You've created slides and videos to illustrate your points. You've prepared your speech. You're ready, or so you thought...

Suddenly, you start imagining every possible disaster. You picture blanking out in front of the audience or fumbling with the slides. You keep replaying past presentations, wondering if you could have done something better. Your throat feels like closing at the thought of what will happen if you make a mistake. And before you know it, a few hours of worrying have passed. Sound familiar?

Or maybe it's something smaller—deciding what to wear for a job interview or a date. Do you go all formal and look like you want it too much? Do you dress casually and possibly create the impression that you aren't interested?

We've all done it. We've all been guilty of overthinking. Yes, sometimes it's helpful and necessary to consider the pros and cons of something. A healthy amount of looking at potential risks is good. But, if you still can't make a decision despite this or take too long considering your options, you're slipping into the trap of overthinking.

The thing is, the more you overthink, the harder it is to make any decisions. Overthinking doesn't help you solve problems. It just keeps you stuck in your head, circling the same issues without getting anywhere.

It's not just that overthinking kills your time, your confidence, and your opportunities. Overthinking can also take your mental health, your sanity. Don't believe me? A quick online search will lead you to numerous studies that link overthinking to anxiety, depression, and even post-traumatic stress disorder (Morin, 2024).

But, more on this later.

For now, understand that overthinking is the process of repeated thoughts over a specific situation or decision. It's often imagining the worst-case scenarios in your future or rehashing past events.

Whatever it is for you, it keeps you stuck. Stuck in a moment you can't escape from. Stuck from enjoying your present. Stuck from living your best life.

Signs You're Overthinking

We all do it. We all overthink at times. I haven't met anyone who enjoys making mistakes or embarrassing themselves. We're only human. But there is a difference between being a productive thinker and an overthinker.

The trick is telling the difference between when your mind is trying to get you ready for something compared to when your thoughts make you anxious.

If you're not sure on which side of the coin you fall, here are a few overthinking signs to look out for:

- **Inability to focus on anything else:** Overthinking can feel like a full-time job. You can't think of anything else. It's difficult to concentrate on another task. Your mind won't let go. You just can't relax.

- **Racing thoughts:** Have you ever laid in bed, desperate for sleep, but your mind is running a marathon? You think about what you need to do, what you didn't do, work deadlines, what someone said to you weeks ago, a face someone made at you, or something you've forgotten. Sometimes, it's a single thought keeping you awake. Other times, it feels like you're trying to think of everything at once.

- **Constant worry and anxiety:** You constantly feel worried and anxious about things completely out of your control, like the weather or others' impression of you. No matter how much you try to stop, you just can't get your anxiety down.

- **Replaying situations:** Overthinking can feel like you're watching the same scene from a movie on repeat. You go over the same decisions and conversations. You replay situations that happened years or even decades ago. Or, you're thinking up hypothetical scenarios of what might happen in the future. You're always wondering how you can be better. But, in doing this, you're not making any changes to improve. You're stuck in a mental loop.

- **Negative self-labels:** How often do you tell yourself you're not good enough? How often do you call yourself a failure? These labels tend to creep into your mind after a setback. These labels thrive on self-doubt, where you start to believe that you aren't able to do anything right. Over time, these limiting beliefs define who you are.

- **Second-guessing yourself:** You're unsure of every decision. This could be something as small as picking a restaurant to eat at or big ones, like choosing a career path. You're continuously going back and forth.

- **Imagining worst-case scenarios:** A minor disagreement with your partner causes you to believe your relationship is falling apart. Or, after making one mistake at work, you believe your career is over. You can't think of anything that could go right, only what could go wrong.

Recognizing the signs of overthinking will help you hit the "pause" button. You'll give yourself the chance to stop the mental spiral before it takes over.

You'll give yourself the power to take back control of your life.

Types of Overthinking

Now that you know how to recognize overthinking in your life, let's turn things upside down: Not all overthinking looks the same.

Yes, you read that correctly. There are many different ways in which you can overthink. They are typically linked to cognitive distortions—basically, negative ways of thinking to either blow things out of proportion or put yourself in the worst possible light.

I'm not going to discuss all possible types of overthinking. Doing that will probably drag you deeper into a pit of endless anxiety. So, let's just look at the three most common ones.

All-Or-Nothing Thinking

This is the type of thinking where things are either perfect or a complete failure. There's no middle ground. It is often called black-and-white thinking, and it can happen in your personal and professional life.

Let's say you're working on a project. You might think, *If I don't get this done perfectly, I'm going to look like a total failure.* You're only focusing on the outcome. You pay no attention to the effort you put in or the progress you make. If it's not perfect, it's not worth it.

Perhaps you want to improve your physical fitness. It goes well until you skip one workout. Instead of seeing it for what it is—one missed workout—your mind goes into overdrive: *I blew it. I'll never be able to stick to this plan, so what's the point?*

The tiniest mistakes can seem like a complete failure. You don't allow yourself to learn from missteps. You judge yourself for them, leaving you stuck in your worries.

Catastrophizing

Catastrophizing happens when you blow things out of proportion. Instead of looking for solutions, you expect the worst possible outcome. You become paralyzed and can't do anything to change the outcome.

Let's look at an example: Your boss gives you negative feedback on a project you're working on. Instead of seeing it as a chance to learn and improve, your mind starts racing: *What if I get fired? If I lose my job, I'll never find another one. I'll end up broke. I'm a complete failure.*

Or, say you have a minor argument with your romantic partner. Perhaps you said something to upset them. Even though it's not a big deal, your mind spirals: *What if they're mad at me? What if this is the beginning of us falling apart? I'll never find someone again. I'll be alone for the rest of my life.*

This thinking sets you up for disaster. Your mind will spiral with fears about things that may never even happen—creating the perfect brewing place for anxiety.

Overgeneralizing

Overgeneralizing is when you apply one bad experience to your entire life. If you struggled to do something once, you believe you'll never be able to do it in the future, no matter how hard you try or improve your skills.

Say you miss a deadline at work. Instead of recognizing that everyone makes mistakes and this is just one incident, your mind races: *I always mess things up. I'll never be successful. This is just how it's always going to be.*

Imagine you're out with friends and someone makes a joke directed at you. It's not a big deal—just a bit of teasing—but your mind starts

19

overgeneralizing: *Great, I'm always the one getting picked on. No one ever takes me seriously.*

With this thinking, you fear the future and worry about things that might never happen. It keeps you stuck in a loop of negativity and self-doubt.

How Overthinking Steals Your Life

Overthinking often starts small. Sometimes, these thoughts seem so insignificant that you don't even notice them. It may just be a quick thought, a worry, or a moment of doubting yourself. But, before you know it, it takes over your entire life. Your mind. Your time. Your confidence. Your opportunities.

Suddenly, everything feels like a massive struggle. You struggle to have fun or relax. It can feel as if you're running a race without any training.

You see, overthinking affects more than just your mental health. It spills over to the rest of your life as well, including your relationships and physical health. It's like a thief that quietly robs you of your life.

Time and Energy Down the Drain

Think about the last time you spent hours overthinking a decision; it could be a job offer, what to say to someone, or even what to cook for dinner.

You're going over every possible scenario, analyzing all the details. You're doing whatever you can to get it perfect. This doesn't bring you closer to taking action. All it does is waste your time and drain you of your energy.

This time and energy could've been used to do something productive. But, instead, you're stuck in neutral, revving your engine loudly without moving an inch forward. You're unable to concentrate on anything else. Your focus remains on your repeating thoughts.

Impact on Decision-Making

Overthinking often leads to what's called "paralysis by analysis." You second-guess every choice. Instead of making a quick decision, you spend hours considering every option. Eventually, you become so overwhelmed by your choices that you can't decide at all.

Let's use the example of buying a house. You've been renting for a while and feel like buying your own place is a step in the right direction. But instead of feeling excited about the idea, you feel completely overwhelmed.

You keep second-guessing every little detail: *Should I go for a fixer-upper or something move-in ready? What if the market crashes after I buy? What if the house needs more repairs than I expect and can afford? What if I regret the decision? What if I can't afford my mortgage?*

21

Instead of making a decision, you end up stuck in the planning phase. You redo your calculations, worry about every possible outcome, and potentially let a good buy slip through your fingers while you're paralyzed by your analysis.

Mental Health: Anxiety and Depression

Even though overthinking isn't a mental illness, it can increase your risk of developing many health conditions, particularly anxiety and depression (Camacho, 2024). A study showed that almost 30% of overthinkers suffer from a combination of depression and anxiety at some point in their lives (Kaiser et al., 2015).

It's difficult to have a positive mindset when you're constantly imagining different worst-case scenarios. It's easy to feel helpless and hopeless when you're always worrying about what might happen.

This negative loop feeds anxiety. The more you worry about the future, the more anxious you become. You start to stress about things you can't control. You become scared of the future. The physical symptoms— like increased heart rate or tightness in your chest—make it even more difficult to calm your racing mind.

Feeling like you're always on edge, replaying past mistakes, or fearing the future can lead to depression. You're so focused on what's wrong and what could go wrong that you can't see solutions or the positives in life.

22

Physical Health: Muscle Tension, Digestive Issues, and Weakened Immune System

Overthinking affects much more than your thoughts and mental health. It can cause physical symptoms as well. The constant worry and stress (we'll go deeper into this a bit later) can result in headaches, body aches, digestive issues, and fatigue (National Institute of Mental Health, 2022).

I'm sure you've picked up or carried something too heavy. Once you put it down (or perhaps a few hours later), you start feeling it in your body. Your back might be sore, your shoulders tight, your neck stiff, or your arms may feel weak.

Now, think of your overthinking as this heavy load you're carrying. After a while, your body will feel like it would after you've carried something heavy. This is because your muscles stay tense during stressful times.

The tension in your body can filter through to all aspects of your life. Say you've been overthinking a project at work. Your muscles will still be in knots by the time you get home, causing you to snap at loved ones for no reason.

The tightness in your body, particularly your neck, can lead to frequent headaches, maybe even migraines (Robinson, 2024b). This can again make you more irritable and drain your patience, which can affect your relationships. You may even isolate yourself, which can add to your depression.

Exhaustion and Disruptive Sleep

Overthinking doesn't only steal your life during the day. It can also steal your sleep at night. You know that feeling of tossing and turning in bed while your mind keeps racing? Sometimes, you're so tired that you manage to fall asleep just to wake up in the middle of the night, your mind filled with worries.

This lack of or interrupted sleep leaves you feeling drained the next day. When you struggle to complete tasks while you're fatigued, self-doubt is bound to take over. This leads to even more overthinking, stress, and anxiety.

The vicious cycle continues: poor sleep makes you fatigued, which makes your mind more prone to overthinking, which disrupts your sleep all the more.

Then, there is the mental exhaustion. This can be just as real and draining as physical fatigue. Constantly staying on the merry-go-round of thoughts that don't get you anywhere will leave you mentally drained.

How Overthinking Rewires Your Brain

We've briefly touched on how overthinking can cause stress, but did you know that this stress can change how your brain functions?

Your brain is made up of billions of neurons that send and receive signals by activating neurotransmitters to create pathways through your body (Robinson, 2024a). Since we aren't all neurosurgeons who understand this easily, let's simplify it even more.

Think about listening to a song. The first time you hear the song, you likely only focus on the melody, the beat, and perhaps a single line in the chorus. The more you listen to it, the more parts of the lyrics you remember until you can eventually sing along. Once you know the song well, you'll likely remember the lyrics for years to come, even if you don't listen to it often.

This is basically what your brain does with thoughts. Every time you have the same thought, the pathways your neurotransmitters create grow stronger. And the stronger these pathways get, the easier it becomes to have specific thoughts. This is why it's so easy to remain trapped in your overthinking. By having repeating thoughts, you're essentially rewiring your brain to continue having them.

But that's not all. Your brain doesn't just process everything you think. It also receives messages through your senses: sight, taste, smell, sound, and touch. When you listen to a song you like, your senses will send messages to your brain to create positive feelings.

Unfortunately, that goes the other way as well. If you have a bad experience with something, your brain will also store the negative emotions. This is why it's so easy to overgeneralize and believe every similar experience in the future will also be bad.

Now, let's add stress to this mix. When you're overthinking, whether it's imagining worst-case scenarios, having catastrophic thoughts, or overgeneralizing events, you'll likely experience high levels of stress and anxiety.

When you stress, your body releases cortisol (Gardener, 2024). This is often called the stress hormone, as it helps your body get ready to fight, flee, or freeze. The purpose of this stress response is to keep you safe when facing danger by helping you make quick or instinctive decisions. This is often called positive stress.

But not all stress has the same effect. Not all stress will keep you safe. If you constantly have high cortisol levels in your body, you'll feel it. You'll be more anxious, have difficulty sleeping, and get sick more frequently.

Chronic stress can also damage and kill cells in the part of your brain responsible for making new memories and controlling emotions (Wright, 2024). This can affect your ability to think, focus, and make decisions. And, as you've probably guessed already, it makes you more prone to overthinking.

The False Sense of Productivity

How often have you sat down on a couch at night, tired after a busy day, but have no idea what you've done all day? You know, those days when you can't cross anything off your to-do list.

That is yet another downside to overthinking. You feel like you're productive all the time because you're thinking of everything: *What should I be doing? What could I be doing? What will happen if I do this? What will happen if I don't do this?*

Sure, it feels like you're busy, but while you're thinking about all the possibilities, you aren't getting anything done.

Simply put, overthinking creates a false sense of productivity.

Now, compare this to when you're productive: You're getting things done. Your mind is focused on the task at hand. You still think before you act, but you make decisions as you go and take action. Instead of running through every possible "what if" scenario, you're finding solutions to problems.

Let's look at the example of wanting more control over your finances. You know you need to review your budget, but you quickly get overwhelmed by the details.

Instead of looking at finding ways to save money and cut expenses, you're reading through the reward options of different credit cards. You're looking up investment options. You're downloading budgeting apps. You go through old receipts, overanalyzing your spending over the past year.

All of these aspects of financial management are good and important if you use them to improve your finances. Unfortunately, it often happens that the extensive research doesn't lead to any positive changes, only to more overthinking.

In the end, you've wasted hours of your time and mental energy overthinking your financial situation without making a single change to your spending habits or increasing your savings.

If you weren't overthinking your finances, the experience could've been completely different. For example, you could've set a single clear goal, something small like cutting down on unnecessary subscriptions or setting up automatic savings of a few dollars a month.

Even if these don't make a massive difference to your finances, it's a step in the right direction. Remember, the key is taking consistent action rather than getting lost in analysis.

Let's look at another example of organizing your home. I'm pretty sure most of us have it: a cupboard or drawer that's so full of junk you can barely close it. Whenever you tidy up, you just shove everything in there to sort out later. Unfortunately, that "later" rarely happens, am I right?

You've finally reached the point where you know you need to tackle that closet. But, instead of taking a garbage bag or sorting bins and getting started, you're overthinking it: You watch organization videos, read books about minimalist living, and make lists of the "perfect" way to sort things.

Sure, you're probably getting great ideas on storage solutions, labels, and systems. But what's the outcome? You've spent hours being "busy," but your junk closet is still a mess.

Instead of overthinking how to organize your space perfectly, you could just decide to do one shelf or drawer a day. Throw away what you no longer need and pack the rest where they belong. This way, you'll get something without being paralyzed by endless options.

The Paralysis of Perfectionism

You might've noticed that I've used the word "perfectly" in this chapter. That's no coincidence. One of the biggest paralyzing factors to overthinking is perfectionism.

When you think about perfectionism, you might picture someone who is obsessed with the finer details or someone whose physical space, be it their desk or home, always looks photoshoot-ready. Perhaps you're

29

thinking of someone beaming with confidence who just knows how to get things done the right way without much effort.

While all of these can be traits of perfectionism, they all stem from one big underlying cause: the fear of not being perfect. It's the fear of falling short. It's that voice in the back of your mind telling you that if you mess up, you're not good enough.

Let's say you've been working for a few years and have had some success along the way, but somehow, you fear it's not good enough. Maybe you feel like you're not earning enough or don't feel fulfilled in your work. You have a great idea for starting your own business. Unfortunately, your overthinking mind has other ideas...

Should I quit my job and go full-time into the business? Or should I keep it as a side hustle? What if it doesn't work out? What if it takes too much time away from my family? What if I make a fool of myself? What if I'm just not cut out to run my own business? What if I make a massive success of it?

You start Googling everything—business plans, marketing strategies, success stories—and by the time you're done, you've spent weeks analyzing it all, but you haven't taken a single step toward your goal.

This is perfectionism at its finest. The fear of getting something wrong, not having every detail in place, or failing paralyzes you. You're so worried about not being perfect that you pause. The longer you wait, the more pressure you feel and the more you question your decisions. In the end, you don't do anything at all.

Let's look at another example: You want to get in better shape. Instead of cutting down on your calories and being more active, you start researching fitness routines, diets, and supplements.

You're looking at which gym has the best equipment, which workout plan is the most effective, and whether you should follow a keto diet or intermittent fasting. You wonder what time of the day would be best to hit the gym and if you really need to take supplements.

But, as soon as you decide what to do, your mind floods with even more questions: *What if I don't stick to it? What if I don't see results right away? What if I look silly in the gym? What if I waste my money? What if I don't make it? What if I fail?*

You're catastrophizing every potential failure. In the end, the idea of not doing it perfectly is so overwhelming that you do nothing at all. You feel safer staying unhappy about your weight and health rather than risk making a mistake. You stay in your comfort zone.

While you may think you're comfortable staying here, let me give you a quick shock: This is the breeding ground for anxiety. You see, anxiety is the fear of something you perceive to be a threat (Chand & Marwaha, 2023). It's a fear that exists in your mind, not necessarily a reality. It's a fear over something that might (or might not) happen in the future.

It's also not just the mistake that causes anxiety. It's what this mistake might mean. Back to our previous example: It's not just a fear of not sticking to a workout routine, making a fool of yourself in the gym, or not sticking to a diet. It's the perception you believe it will create: feeling or looking incompetent or incapable. It's showing others—and yourself—that you aren't perfect.

So, what is the key to breaking free from your perfectionism? As simple and perhaps obvious as it may sound, it's all about recognizing that perfection doesn't exist. Never has, and never will.

Life is messy. Nothing you ever do will be flawless. You will stumble, but that's part of the process. That's part of being a human being.

Instead of seeing your imperfections as flaws, make the mindset shift to see them as characteristics. These are the quirks that make you unique. It's a lot easier to embrace your characteristics than perceived flaws.

Chapter Takeaways

- Overthinking is constantly thinking about something to the point where it takes control of your mind and life. It causes paralysis as you replay situations and second-guess yourself. This fuels anxiety and stress.

- While there are many different types of overthinking, the three most common ones are:

- All-or-nothing thinking is the belief that things are either perfect or a complete failure.

- Catastrophizing involves blowing minor problems out of proportion and expecting the worst possible outcome.

- Overgeneralizing is when one bad experience is applied to everything else in your life.

- Over time, overthinking steals your entire life. It drains your time and energy and disrupts your sleep.

- When you're overthinking, you always feel busy, but you're not getting much done. As a result, it creates a false sense of productivity.

- Overthinking and perfectionism are closely linked: You avoid taking action because you fear not doing it perfectly.

***

Understanding your overthinking and the impact it has on your life lays a good foundation for finding ways to address it for good. In the next chapter, we'll identify your overthinking triggers to help you stop these thoughts before they spiral out of control.

CHAPTER 2

Identifying Your Overthinking Triggers (So You Can Shut Them Down)

There is hope, even when your brain tells you there isn't.

–John Green

Can you remember the last time you were overthinking? Can you remember exactly what you were thinking about? I'm not talking about all the thoughts that filled your mind. I'm talking about the original one. The thought that started it all.

Perhaps it wasn't a specific thought. Maybe something happened that made you feel unsure of yourself. It may be something that happened on that day or perhaps even years ago. Or maybe it's anxiety over something that might happen in the future.

You see, your overthinking can be triggered by basically anything. Someone might look at you in a way that causes you to overthink. You might smell something that makes you think back to a time you didn't feel comfortable. Or, it can even be that you're overthinking so often

34

that you can't remember a time when your thoughts weren't all over the place.

Whatever the case is for you, ask yourself if there is any pattern to your overthinking. Perhaps there are certain situations, people, or events that trigger you. If you can't identify a pattern or trigger yet, don't stress. Trust me, you will get there!

Next, think of your physical body while you're overthinking. How does your body react? Do you feel tension in your shoulders? Is your heart racing? Do you struggle to take a deep breath? Is your stomach in knots? Are you sweating more than normal? Are you feeling exhausted without doing anything to make you tired?

You may wonder why I'm asking you all these questions. You may even start to feel a bit uncomfortable with some of them. That's exactly the point: not to make you uncomfortable, but to make you more aware.

You see, many signs can help you recognize your overthinking. The more you become aware of how you respond to your thoughts, the easier it will be to identify your triggers.

Now, let's get into it: What is a trigger?

You've probably heard the term before, but what does it mean when it comes to overthinking? A trigger is simply something that causes you to react. It's something that pulls you into a cycle of stress, worry, or doubt, often without even realizing it.

Whether it's an uncomfortable conversation, the pressure to perform at work, trauma from the past, or even feeling unsure about the future, these triggers cause your mind to spiral.

When you know what triggers your overthinking, you'll know when you need to do something to stop your mind from spiraling. It will help you realize what strategies you need to implement to manage those moments. Knowing your triggers will help you regain control.

The Big Stress Triggers

Every person has their own triggers for overthinking based on their experiences (past and present), emotions, and insecurities.

They don't necessarily need to have negative causes. You may be triggered into overthinking by your aspirations and goals as well, especially when you have big hopes for your future.

What triggers your overthinking might also not affect others. What causes you sleepless nights of continuous thinking and worrying might not faze someone else in the slightest, and vice versa.

Luckily, there are many ways you can identify what causes your mind to race. One of these is to look at your stress levels. Remember when we discussed (in Chapter 1) how stress and overthinking are closely linked?

Let's look at some of the biggest causes of stress. They may not all apply to your life, but reading through these may increase your awareness.

I encourage you to keep a notepad or notes app on your phone close to jot down anything that stands out and may apply to you. This will be very helpful later when we do our 10-minute exercise on identifying your triggers to overthinking.

Relationships and Family Responsibilities

Let's start with the stress you may experience in your relationships and family connections. As much as your loved ones should bring peace and joy to your life, this isn't always as simple. These connections can often be a silent weight on your shoulders.

You may feel like your entire life is a juggling act. You're balancing work, your romantic partner, your family obligations, and your friends while you still need to make time for yourself as well.

Let's break down the most common sources of stress in your family responsibilities:

- **Your romantic relationship:** You may feel pressure to maintain a "perfect" relationship with your partner. Unfortunately, many relationships that look good to outsiders might be a completely different story in reality. There's just no such thing as a perfect relationship.

- **Your role as a parent:** If you have children, you'll likely know a whole different brand of stress. Your days are filled with managing their schedules, making sure they do enough extracurricular activities, and helping them with schoolwork. And it doesn't end there! You're also constantly worried about their well-being and future.

- **Other family dynamics:** You may still be lucky enough to have parents, but as they get older, you worry about their future: financially, emotionally, mentally, and health-wise. You may also butt heads with siblings or have had to deal with the death of a loved one.

- **Strained relationships:** The stress of going through a breakup or divorce or even being estranged from family members can be overwhelming. Even losing friendships can cause your stress levels to rise.

Financial Concerns

Money can be a major cause of worry. You may look at your bank account and wonder where your money has disappeared to. Maybe you just don't know how to cut your monthly expenses. Or, perhaps looking at your retirement savings causes you anxiety.

Some of the most common causes of financial stress include:

- **Managing debt:** You may constantly struggle to pay off your debt, whether it's credit cards, a car loan, or a mortgage. No matter how much you pay toward them, your outstanding balances don't seem to go down. It's frustrating.

- **Daily budgets:** Once your debt is paid, you may wonder where you'll find enough money to pay your daily bills and buy basic needs like groceries. This stress can eat away at you.

- **Insufficient savings:** You might worry that you won't be able to retire comfortably or have enough savings for your children's education.

- **Insurance:** Apart from the monthly costs we've already mentioned, you need to keep money aside for healthcare and ensure you have the right insurance coverage.

Career Challenges

You likely spend the majority of your life at work. Sure, if you do something you enjoy, you may not mind spending so much of your time at the office. Unfortunately, work can also be a significant cause of stress and anxiety.

Let's look at some of the work stresses you might experience:

- **Pressures at work:** Whether you're managing tight deadlines, dealing with multiple projects, or working in a fast-paced environment, your stress can seem never-ending. You might be constantly under pressure to perform, which can cause burnout.

- **Feeling unappreciated:** Feeling like your hard work isn't noticed can be very demotivating. You may begin to question your worth and whether you're on the right career path.

- **Lack of career progression:** Maybe you feel like your career is moving forward as planned, especially if you've been in the same position for years. It's easy to get caught up in a mindset of *Is this it?*

- **Losing your job:** There may be many reasons why you fear losing your job. It can be due to company downsizing or your performance. Regardless of the reason, the thought of losing your source of income can be terrifying.

- **Starting a new job:** The excitement of new opportunities can often be filled with anxiety. When you start a new job, you may feel like you need to prove yourself, learn new systems, and build relationships all at once.

Lack of Personal Time

Not having enough time for yourself can cause stress you may not notice immediately. Some of these stressors can include:

- **Balancing your roles:** You have many different roles: a partner, a parent, a provider, or an employee. This leaves little time for yourself.

- **Your identity:** You might find yourself asking, *Who am I?* or *What do I enjoy doing?* This feeling of losing touch with your true self can be very stressful.

Health

Health challenges can always be a big cause of stress. As you get older, your body will give you more and more hints that you're not invincible.

Let's look at some common health concerns that may keep you awake at night:

- **Staying in shape:** You may have less time and energy for workouts, and your metabolism slows down as you get older. The risk of injury during workouts increases.

- **Long-term health issues:** High blood pressure, cholesterol, and other health concerns may leave you with more questions than answers. You may worry that these are only the start of serious conditions.

- **Lifestyle choices:** You know you should eat better, work out more, and get enough sleep, but when you're working long hours and managing family responsibilities, it's difficult to put time and effort into your lifestyle choices.

Fear of Failure

This is a trigger we've discussed in Chapter 1 already, but it's worth another mention because it affects many overthinkers. This fear can completely change how you see success.

You start to believe anything short of perfection is unacceptable. When you fear failure, you struggle to see possibilities and solutions. Your focus is only on potential worst-case scenarios and how to avoid them.

Regrets

When you look back at the choices you've made in the past, it's easy to second-guess some. Unfortunately, thinking about these regrets can cause you to doubt your future decisions as well.

Some of these causes of stress can include:

- **The "what-ifs":** It's natural to wonder how things could've been different if you made other decisions. This can leave you feeling stuck and afraid.

- **Unnecessary comparisons:** You might find yourself comparing your life to others—friends, colleagues, even strangers on social media—and wondering if you've somehow fallen behind.

- **Expecting control:** Regrets often come from the idea that you had control over every outcome. The reality is that life is messy and unpredictable, and in many cases, there was nothing you could've done to change the results.

Deeply Rooted Negative Beliefs

Deeply rooted negative beliefs often come from past experiences, whether it's childhood trauma, previous relationships, or challenging moments in life. If you deal with these events as they happen, you can put them behind you. But, if you don't, they can result in negative beliefs about yourself.

These are those repeating things you tell yourself. *I'm not good enough. I'll never be successful. I'll always be alone. I'll always be a failure.*

These negative beliefs are rarely true, but they can be difficult to shake because they are tied to strong emotions such as fear, shame, or guilt. It's easy to feel like they define you.

Over time, these beliefs can lead to chronic stress, as you're constantly doubting yourself. They make you question everything about yourself and your decisions.

You might feel like you're constantly walking on eggshells, terrified that one misstep will confirm that deep-rooted belief. You feel like one mistake will show yourself and the world you're not good enough. It's exhausting.

43

People-Pleasing

The pressure of meeting the expectations of others can be a lot. Those expectations leave you feeling like you're constantly playing catch-up, like you're always working your butt off to please others.

You may say yes to things when you'd rather say no because you're worried about what others will think. This adds extra stress and can easily lead to overthinking. What makes your stress even worse is that while you're busy trying to please others, you forget about your own needs. You push yourself past your limits.

Eventually, people-pleasing can cause you to resent others. It may show up as frustration over not having time for yourself or feeling like others are taking you for granted.

Major Life Events

Significant changes in your life can sometimes be the biggest triggers of stress. When you think of major life events, you'll likely think of moving to a new city, getting married, having a child, or even changing jobs.

But it can also be something smaller, like dealing with difficult neighbors or caring for a sick family member. It can be any situation you find yourself in where there are many uncertainties.

The Impact of Past Traumas

We all have a past. We've all had something happen that we wish never did. This moment could be something seemingly insignificant to others, like being laughed at during a high-pressure situation. Or, it can be more serious, like being abused.

Your past can leave lasting scars. You may not always be aware of how it affects you. You may also be unwilling to even admit to yourself that you're traumatized. You may even believe others won't get why you're still upset over something that happened in the past.

Whatever it may be, you may find yourself overthinking as a trauma response. Yes, you read correctly. You may be using overthinking as a way of coping.

Before we go any deeper into this—and yes, this section may leave you feeling uncomfortable—let's first look at exactly what is meant by the phrase "trauma response" (Tanasugarn, 2024).

At the risk of oversimplifying it, it's basically how you respond—physically, emotionally, and mentally—to something based on a past trauma. It's where your body and brain use your previous experiences to create your survival instincts.

Now, you may wonder how these survival instincts differ from the typical fight, flight, or freeze response everyone experiences during stressful times. The answer is simple: The stress response is designed to keep you safe when your brain perceives a threat.

Your trauma response isn't necessarily to keep you safe, although it can be the case. For example, if your previous trauma was being bullied, your trauma response will activate your body to try to avoid more bullying in the future.

But the primary purpose of this response is to prevent a similar trauma from happening again. So, if you've failed at completing a specific project in the past, your trauma response may be to deliberately make you doubt yourself to such an extent that you refuse to take on a similar project again.

This is where overthinking can become a trauma response: Your mind is taking you through thought cycles to keep you away from what you fear the most. You're using overthinking as a coping mechanism to protect yourself from more hurt and disappointment.

This is especially common for people who experienced some sort of childhood trauma (Illinois Recovery Center, 2024). Say you grew up in an environment where you were often criticized or didn't feel emotionally supported. Your overthinking might be a way for you to gain a sense of control or safety. It's a way to make sure things "go right" or avoid making mistakes.

Unfortunately, using this as a trauma response won't help you to deal with what happened to you. It's more of a band-aid that you put on a wound rather than treating the wound so that it can heal. While covering your "wound," you're stuck in a cycle of analyzing, second-guessing, and trying to predict outcomes.

Remember in the previous chapter when we discussed how overthinking can rewire your brain? Trauma can take this even a step further. If you don't effectively deal with your trauma, your brain will be wired to stay on high alert (Frederick, 2019). This means that you'll constantly be on the lookout for danger. If overthinking is your trauma response, you'll always be ready for your mind to spiral out of control.

You'll overthink every detail. You'll plan for worst-case scenarios. You'll rehash past mistakes. You'll do all of this to make sure you're not caught off guard again.

Does this make you feel safe? Sure it does. Is it healthy? Most definitely not.

By continuing with overthinking as a trauma response, mental exhaustion will be inevitable. The chronic stress will take a toll on your physical health as well.

The Three-Question Rule

Remember when I promised this book wouldn't be filled with B.S. I'm not here to tell you that you can or should stop yourself from thinking altogether. You're a human being. You will have thoughts. It's natural.

We aren't here to try to turn you into a robot. We are here to help you stop overthinking, not for a few days or weeks, but for good.

So, how do you do this? How do you accept that having thoughts is a natural part of life but stop these thoughts from taking control of your mind?

It's all about determining which thoughts are helpful and which aren't. Sounds simple, hey? Unfortunately, it can be easier said than done.

You see, when your mind is spiraling, you'll make yourself believe that every thought you have is important. You'll believe every thought is productive and helpful. You'll even believe every thought is true.

But I can assure you, it's not.

This is where the three-question rule comes in. When you catch your mind spiraling out of control, simply ask yourself these questions: *Is it true? Is it helpful? Is it kind?*

Let's unpack this.

Is It True?

Start by asking yourself: *Is this thought true?*

One of the biggest mistakes you can make is believing every thought you have is true. Just because something pops into your head doesn't mean there is any evidence to substantiate it. It's not always based on facts. Sometimes, it's based on assumptions.

Let's say you're overthinking a conversation you had with your boss. You're going over every detail, believing that somewhere, you'll find proof that you've messed up. Take a moment to pause. Did you really make a mistake? Or did you perhaps misinterpret the conversation?

What other possibilities might there be? Perhaps you were feeling stressed and blocked out any positive things that were said. Maybe your boss was in a rush and didn't explain themselves properly. Maybe there are many other possibilities.

Once you start to really look at the different possibilities, you may be surprised at how often your mind spirals on assumptions. Differentiating between the lies and truths is key to overcoming your overthinking.

If your thought is based on assumptions, you can acknowledge it, remind yourself that it's not a fact, and move on.

Is It Helpful?

The second question is: *Is this thought helping me?* Just because a thought is true doesn't mean you should allow it to take over. Even a thought based on facts can keep you stuck.

Let's look at this example: You want to get into shape, but whenever you think about starting a new fitness routine, negative thoughts fill your mind: *I'm just not good at this. I've tried exercising already, and it wasn't for me.*

Even though you have struggled in the past, is it helping you to hold onto that? Does this not push you to give up before you even try? Does this give you a chance to improve?

Now, think about how you can reframe this into a helpful thought. Maybe it could look something like this: *I might not enjoy working out, but I can do this. I can take small steps to get there.* It moves you forward, even if it's just one small action, like going for a walk.

The key is to realize when your thoughts are keeping you paralyzed and then changing them to help you move forward. It's about challenging yourself to change the thoughts that used to hold you back into ones that encourage you to take action.

Is It Kind?

Finally, ask yourself: *Is this thought kind?*

When you're busy overthinking, it's easy to fall into the trap of negative self-talk. I'm sure this won't shock you, but beating yourself up isn't healthy. It's not helping you to feel better about yourself. It's not helping you to move forward. It's just adding to your stress.

Think about a time when you felt bad about yourself. Let's say you forgot about an important date, like a wedding anniversary, and now you find yourself in the dog house. Your mind may start to spiral: *I always mess things up. My partner is now going to leave me. I'm useless and will be single forever.*

Now, ask yourself if this is really the best way to deal with the situation. Are your thoughts kind? Are they building you up and helping you move forward? Or are they dragging you down, making you feel stuck?

Now, here is a question I encourage you to ask yourself when your thoughts get the better of you: Would you say that to a best friend? If not, why do you speak to yourself like that?

How can you change that thought into something more productive? Maybe it could look something like: *I made a mistake, but it's not the end of the world. I can make up for it. I can still show my partner how much they mean to me. Everything will be okay.*

Kindness can go a long way, as we'll discuss in more detail in Chapter 8. Always remember to give yourself some grace. Making mistakes is part of being human. It's your choice what thoughts you allow to linger. Are they thoughts that hold you back or push you forward?

10-Minute Exercise: Track Your Triggers

Now that you have a better idea of what might be triggering your overthinking, let's put it into practice. In this first 10-minute exercise, we'll focus on tracking your overthinking triggers and patterns to help you realize when you need to pull yourself out of the spiral before it becomes overwhelming.

Step 1: Identify Your Overthinking

The next time you find yourself getting stuck in your thoughts, write down the following:

- **What triggered the overthinking?** Did something happen at work? Was it a conversation? Did you have to make a difficult decision?

- **When did it happen?** What time of the day was it? What was happening in your life at that moment?

- **How did it make you feel?** Did you experience any strong emotions, like feeling anxious, overwhelmed, or frustrated?

- **What thoughts kept repeating?** Did you have many "what if" questions? Were you imagining the worst-case scenario?

Let's look at an example:

- **Trigger:** The company I work for is restructuring. I worry that I might lose my job.

- **Time:** Around 3 p.m. at work. I was stressed after receiving feedback from my boss.

- **Feelings:** I was feeling anxious and frustrated because the feedback didn't go as I anticipated it would.

- **Repeating thoughts**: What if they fire me? What if I can't find another job? What if I can't support my family? What if I lose everything?

Step 2: Use the Three-Question Rule

Now, use the three-question rule to help you deal with these thoughts:

- **Is this true?**
  - Am I actually at risk of losing my job? Although the company is restructuring, no one suggested I might be fired.

- **Is it helpful?**
  - The worst-case scenario would be getting fired, but my boss gave me positive feedback last week, and I have many skills the company needs.
  - Even if there are layoffs, I have connections that could help me find another job. It's not hopeless.

- **Is it kind? What would you say to a friend?**
  - Fearing that I might lose my job isn't good for my self-confidence.
  - I would encourage a friend to continue doing their best work to show their value.

Step 3: Reflect on Your Answers

Now, take a moment to reflect on your answers. This will help you understand how to reframe your thoughts to reduce your stress and overthinking.

- **Trigger**: I'm worried about losing my job.

- **Is this based on facts or assumptions?** I'm assuming I could get laid off, but at the moment, there's no evidence that this is a fact.

- **Most likely outcome?** It's more likely that I'm worried over nothing. I got one set of negative feedback, and the rest have been good. I don't think I should stress about this.

- **What action can I take?** I'll ask for a one-on-one with my boss to talk about my performance in general. If the meeting goes well, I'll ask about the company's plans to ease my mind.

Chapter Summary

- Overthinking is triggered by experiences, fears, and insecurities. It's different for everyone and can be caused by both negative and positive stressors.

- Some of the common causes of stress and overthinking include relationships and family responsibilities, finances, career challenges, lack of personal time, health issues, fear of failure, regrets, past traumas, people-pleasing, and major life events.

- You need to figure out if your thoughts are holding you back and keeping you stuck or pushing you forward. You can do this by using the three-question rule:

  - Is it true?

  - Is it helpful?

  - Is it kind?

***

Understanding why you overthink is key to overcoming this habit, but it's only the first step. In the next section, we'll look at how you can rewire your mind to end your overthinking, starting with shifting from passive worry to intentional thinking. Keep reading; you're well on your way to breaking this cycle for good!

PART 2

Rewiring Your Mind to End Overthinking

CHAPTER 3

The Mindset Shift That Ends Overthinking

You will never be free until you free yourself from the prison of your own false thoughts.

–Philip Arnold

I remember the first time I had an anxiety attack.

It was my 30th birthday celebration with a few friends and my girlfriend. I was having some drinks and laughs. I was having a great time surrounded by the people I love.

Then, all of a sudden, I couldn't breathe. It started small, like a subtle tightening in my chest. Before I could make sense of what was happening, my heart was racing. I tried to grab onto something—anything—to calm myself, but nothing worked. I could feel my breath getting shorter. I kept panting. It was embarrassing.

These anxiety attacks continued for the next year. I was under *a lot* of stress.

It all started when I decided to switch careers at the end of 2019. You always hear people say, "Go after your dreams." That's exactly what I did. I went into youth motivational speaking. But, before I could find my feet, the pandemic hit. I wasn't ready for the suffering that followed.

I barely had an income for the next two and a half years. I was doing odd jobs. I used up my entire savings account. I was borrowing money from family. I was completely broke. I was a complete mess, barely surviving.

All my life, I've struggled with anxiety, spurred on by my perfectionism, people-pleasing, and overthinking. But my sudden financial downfall made it 10 times worse.

My confidence was shattered. I could've completely quit my dream. That would've been the easy way out. I could've easily allowed myself to fall into the trap of the "what if" questions swirling in my mind.

What if I never make it out of this hole? What if I'm going to fail again? What if I lose even more?

Do you want to hear the good news? None of my "what-ifs" came true. Instead of allowing my overthinking to destroy my life, I took a short break from my business to gain clarity.

A couple of years later, I continued pursuing my dreams. Instead of just doing motivational speeches, I focused my attention on motivating people through my writing. I published my first self-help book in 2020.

Most self-published authors don't sell more than 200 copies in a book's lifetime. I passed that within the first few months.

After seeing the impact my book had on the lives of so many people years later, I decided to write more books. When I made that decision, I could've easily fallen into my overthinking trap. But I didn't.

Because I still needed to earn income, I also took on a full-time job I loved. My days were full. The easy option would've been to be content with what I had and leave it at that. The fear of failing again was constant. I doubted myself daily. On so many days, I wanted to give up.

But, somehow, I managed to push through. I realized that each failure and tough moment comes with valuable lessons and insights. Instead of dwelling on negative "what-ifs," I changed the narrative to: What if I could make it work? What if this time is different?

This change in mindset helped me realize that I could make it work. So can you.

Never let past negative experiences define your current actions. Just because you had a failed business, a failed relationship, or a failed attempt at a goal doesn't mean you will always be a failure.

Overthinking is just something you do. It doesn't have to define you. It doesn't have to dictate your future.

Overthinking Is a Habit

If you've been overthinking for a long time, you might struggle to remember a time when your mind didn't spiral out of control. You may feel like it's part of who you are, like a personality trait you can't seem to shake.

What if I tell you it's not an inherent part of your being? It's just a habit. Nothing more, nothing less.

Before we go any further, let's start by understanding habits. Simply put, it's small, repeated actions you do daily. It's those things you do automatically. Research from Duke University shows that habits account for around 40% of your daily behaviors (Clear, 2018).

Think about something you do without thinking. Perhaps you're a smoker. You don't actively think about it every time you light a cigarette or pull your vape out. You just do it.

Or, a healthy habit: brushing your teeth. You likely don't have to remind yourself to brush your teeth in the mornings before you leave home. It's not a choice you make. You do it without thinking.

The first few times you've done this action, you decided to do it. There was a time when smoking didn't come naturally to you, and when you were a youngster, your parents or caregivers had to remind you to brush your teeth.

The more you did this action, the easier it became to do it or remember to do it. Over time, it became a cycle, one you fall into and do without even realizing it.

The same goes for overthinking. Even though you probably never decided that you wanted to overthink, it served a purpose. It brought some benefit to your life. You might have believed you were simply carefully thinking things through, or in the case of a trauma response, you might've tried to avoid getting hurt or disappointed.

The more you did it, the stronger the urge to overthink became. Before you knew it, it became a habit. Your mind now goes into overthinking mode automatically. You don't decide to spend hours analyzing the same thought, situation, or conversation. You just do it.

To help people understand their habits, author Charles Duhigg introduced the concept of a habit loop (2012). He explains that every habit has three parts: the cue (or trigger), the routine (or behavior), and the reward.

Let's put this into an overthinking example: Your cue or trigger might be related to stress, uncertainty, or a fear of making the wrong choice. Maybe it's a big presentation you're preparing for at work. The stress of needing to get it right triggers the overthinking pattern.

You begin to mentally replay scenarios, question every possible outcome, and second-guess your decisions. This mental spiral is the routine or behavior that follows your trigger—analyzing, overanalyzing, and overcompensating.

And the reward? It's the temporary relief that comes from feeling like you've considered every angle, even though deep down, you know it's not actually helping.

This habit loop becomes automatic. Your brain doesn't question why you're doing it; it just does it because that has become your go-to way of coping. And the reward, whether real or healthy, strengthens the habit.

Now, here is the good news: All habits can be broken. Just like you've trained your brain to overthink, you can retrain it to break free from the cycle.

Yes, it may not be easy. If you've ever tried to break a strong habit, you'll know exactly what I'm talking about. Many people can break strong habits daily, whether it's smoking, unhealthy lifestyles, excessive screen time, or overthinking.

If they can, why can't you? If I could stop overthinking, what's keeping you from doing this? You can stop your habit of overthinking and regain control of your mind.

Stack Your Overthinking With a Positive Habit

I've said it before, and I'll say it again: Breaking a strong habit can be difficult. I'm not trying to discourage you here. I'm simply keeping to my promise: There is no B.S. in this book.

Acknowledging that you may struggle can sometimes be half the battle won. You won't go into this believing you'll get it right the very first time. You go into this with a realistic mindset.

So, if your overthinking is a habit that you do automatically, almost on autopilot, how can you stop it? How do you break this cycle?

The first step is awareness. Remember the triggers that we've discussed in the previous chapter? Your triggers, or cues, are the start of your overthinking cycle, or habit loop. Identifying them is key.

Once you've identified the cue, it's time to go to the second step: changing the routine. Instead of diving into overthinking, try setting a time limit for yourself. For example, say something like, "I'll spend ten minutes thinking about this, then I'm moving on."

Or, you can try reframing the situation. While Chapter 2's three-question rule is very helpful with this, you can also try another approach: Instead of focusing on all the potential negative outcomes, ask yourself: *What's the worst that could happen if I make a mistake? What would be the worst-case scenario here?*

Often, the fear of failure is what keeps you stuck in the loop. But, once you realize that mistakes are a part of life and usually lead to growth or that your fears are highly unlikely to become a reality, it gets easier to break free from this cycle.

The third step is about getting a better reward. Our brains are wired to seek rewards. To break any habit, you need to replace the old reward with something better. In the case of overthinking, your rewards will be instant but short-term. They won't help you going forward. They only make you feel better in that moment.

Think of different rewards that will have a prolonged effect on your life. Perhaps it can be the satisfaction of doing something productive, whether it's sending an email, having a conversation, or making a decision.

It could be the relief of not doing mental gymnastics and actually doing something, even if it isn't perfect.

Unfortunately, there may be times when you feel like you're failing, no matter how hard you try to break your habit loop. It feels like you're taking one step forward and two steps backward.

I've been there. I know how difficult it can be. This is why I'm bringing you another solution: If you can't seem to break your habit loop, why not use it to build better habits?

Yes, you read correctly: You can use your overthinking to your advantage.

The key to doing this is called habit stacking, a concept initially introduced by productivity author S.J. Scott (2014). It's quite simple to do: Habit stacking is all about taking a habit you already do daily and stacking a new behavior on top of it. This way, you don't have to create a whole new routine from scratch. You're simply adding a new habit to an old one, making it easier to stick with.

So, how does this work? How can this be a game-changer in stopping your overthinking if the whole premise of habit stacking is to continue with the old habit?

It comes down to how your brain works. In Chapter 1, we discussed how your brain's neurons form pathways when you do things repeatedly. This is basically how a habit is formed. While you're creating these new connections, your brain essentially gets rid of the ones you no longer use. This process is called synaptic pruning.

When you stack a new habit on top of an existing one, you won't force your brain to create new pathways. You're simply making use of one that already exists (Perry, 2024).

As this new habit gets stronger, your brain will either create a separate pathway for it or, in the case of habit stacking, change the existing pathway you're using.

Let's look at an example of how this can work for overthinking:

1. **Trigger**: The moment you catch yourself overthinking—whether it's about work, a personal issue, or something that feels off—change your environment. This can be stepping outside for a few minutes, going for a quick walk, or perhaps even just standing if you were sitting down.

2. **New habit**: Moving. That's it. Just a simple walk to change your environment and get your body moving. By doing this, you'll reset your brain. Whether it's getting fresh air to help you think clearly or seeing something to distract you, movement helps reset your brain.

3. **Reward**: Now, here's the important part: What do you get out of this? As you walk, your thoughts will change. The fresh air, the change of scenery, and the physical activity interrupt your overthinking. It's like hitting your brain's "reset" button. This movement will also increase your heart rate, boosting blood flow to your brain, which helps you to think more clearly. Then, there are the secondary or sometimes unexpected rewards of improved health from being more active and getting into shape.

Plus, walking will give your mind permission to stop obsessing. When you return, you're more likely to approach whatever's on your mind with a fresh perspective and ideas.

It's as simple as that. Really.

When I first heard of habit stacking, I had my doubts about whether it would help. I even overanalyzed it, reading as much literature on it as I could instead of just giving it a try. Luckily, I eventually decided to do it. To my surprise, this was a game changer.

I can already hear you ask the next question: *How will this help me stop overthinking for good?*

The answer lies in the reward. Remember what we discussed above about our brains always seeking the best possible reward?

If you can make sure your reward for your new habit is better, perhaps longer lasting than the slight benefit overthinking will bring, your brain will create a stronger pathway to this new habit. Eventually, it will either completely change or replace the overthinking pathways that exist in your brain.

Perhaps simply getting fresh air or being more active isn't a good enough reward for you to change your old habit. But, if you dig a little deeper, you'll see that moving can bring many other rewards as well. I've already mentioned improved health and getting into shape. But, as you move, you can have a quick chat with people you see along the way, breaking any isolation you might have felt. Physical activity can also help to improve your sleep at night. And realizing you can break your cycle of overthinking will boost your confidence.

It's important to choose a behavior and reward that work for you. If you don't enjoy physical exercise, going for a walk definitely won't be a good enough reward. Always choose something aligned with your interests.

When you think of rewards, the possibilities can be endless. Your new habit will become automatic. Your brain will be trained to notice when you're overthinking and immediately tell your body to start moving. It's as simple as that.

Create the Right Mindset With Healthy Habits

Breaking your habit of overthinking, either by stopping your habit loop or stacking a positive habit on top of your overanalyzing, is a good first step. Next, consider starting a few healthy habits. These are the types of habits that will help you create a strong and resilient mindset to stop your overthinking for good.

Think of this as building a house. Before you can even think of building walls, adding windows, putting on a roof, and decorating it, you need a solid foundation. If you don't take care of your foundation, your house won't last. Your walls will crack. Your roof will start to sag until it eventually tumbles in.

Your mindset is this foundation. This mindset will help you focus on solutions rather than the problem. It will help you embrace uncertainty by knowing that these moments hold countless possibilities. It will help you feel ready to take action and prevent overthinking for controlling your thoughts and decisions.

In essence, healthy habits are the concrete and rebar in your mindset, two crucial materials for creating a strong foundation.

Let's look at some habits that can help you move away from overthinking and toward clarity:

- **Create a good morning routine:** If you start your day right, you'll feel ready for any challenges you may face during the day. It could be as simple as making a to-do list in the morning, having a quick meditation session, or even making your bed as soon as you get up.

- **Get enough sleep:** When you feel well-rested, you'll find it easier to deal with the challenges you'll face during the day. Create a set routine of going to bed and waking up at the same time, even over weekends. This will help to set your body's internal clock, which helps you fall asleep more easily. Reduce your screen time for at least an hour before you want to go to bed to boost your body's production of melatonin, the hormone that helps you fall asleep. Create a cool, dark environment, and if need be, use a white noise machine to block out external noise.

- **Watch your diet:** What you put into your body has a big impact on how you feel mentally. If you eat a lot of junk food, you'll struggle to think clearly. Eating a balanced diet with plenty of fruits, vegetables, and whole grains can help regulate your mood and boost your energy.

- **Be more active:** Exercise is about more than building muscle. It's also about clearing your head. I've already mentioned that physical activity increases the blood flow to your brain, but it also releases feel-good endorphins. This can help reduce stress and anxiety.

- **Focus on what you can control:** Overthinking thrives on uncertainty. Many of the things you stress and overthink about are likely not things you can control. Let's say you're stuck in traffic on your way to work. You can't control it; you will be late for work. But what you *can* control is how you handle yourself. Perhaps it's taking a different route, calling ahead, or rescheduling an early meeting.

- **Take care of yourself:** Sometimes, the best thing you can do is make time for yourself. Self-care is so important, and you should never feel guilty about taking a few minutes to do something you enjoy. This could be something as simple as making time to read a book, watch a show, work in the garden, or even spend a few minutes longer in the shower.

Always remember that the purpose of these habits isn't to completely cut stress and doubt from your life. That's just not possible. It's about becoming resilient enough to handle the mental noise of overthinking with more ease.

10-Minute Exercise: Replace Your Negative Habits

Time for another 10-minute exercise! This time, we're going to look at replacing more of your negative habits with positive ones to build a strong mindset to end your overthinking.

Step 1: List Your Negative Habits That Trigger Overthinking

Make a note of at least three habits you want to replace. Here are some examples to get you thinking:

- checking emails or social media first thing in the morning and getting caught up in unnecessary drama

- watching too much news or reading about negative things

- overanalyzing everything you've said and done during the day

- saying yes every time someone asks you to do something

Step 2: List Some Positive Habits

Write down at least three positive habits that can help you stop overthinking. Here are a few examples:

- practicing mindfulness or meditation (We'll discuss this in the next chapter.)

- going for a walk after lunch to clear your mind

- adding "no work" time in the evenings to focus on your hobbies, a side hustle, or spending time with family

- practicing gratitude by writing down three things you're thankful for every day

- journaling before bed to reflect on the day

Step 3: Replace Negative Habits With Positive Ones

Pick one negative habit from your list and either replace it with a positive one or stack the healthy habit on it. Here are a few examples:

- If you overthink in the mornings, start your day with a five-minute meditation. This will help you feel more grounded in the present moment and less likely to get lost in your thoughts.

- If you overanalyze at night, journal about the positives of your day to help you feel good before you climb into bed.

- If you're always saying yes to everything, try setting clear boundaries and saying no when needed. We'll discuss this in more detail in Chapter 6.

Step 4: Track Your Progress

After a week, check in with yourself. Ask yourself questions like:

- How often was I able to replace my negative habits?

- What went well?

- What could I improve on for next week?

Step 5: Give Yourself Credit

After doing this consistently for a month, give yourself a high-five. You've taken a major step in breaking the cycle of overthinking. Even if it wasn't perfect, pat yourself of the back for doing your best.

If you still struggle, remind yourself that this is not a race. Focus on one habit at a time and build your way up.

Chapter Summary

- Overthinking isn't part of who you are. It's a habit that formed over time. It's something you taught yourself to do, so it's something you can teach yourself *not* to do.

- The habit loop consists of three parts: cue (trigger), routine (overthinking), and reward (temporary relief).

- Just like any habit, overthinking can be broken by being more aware of your thoughts and replacing the old reward with something better.

- Habit stacking can be very effective in breaking old habits. To do this, you stack a new habit (like walking) on top of your overthinking. Over time, you disrupt your overthinking and reset your brain.

- Building healthy habits can help to create a strong mindset to stop overthinking for good.

***

Creating positive habits and letting go of unhealthy ones is a good start to creating the mindset to stop overthinking. Unfortunately, there will still be times when your mind spirals without you even realizing it. This is where being more mindful in your daily life can make a massive difference. In the next chapter, we'll look at the impact mindfulness can make in your life, as well as how you can reduce unnecessary mental clutter and learn to trust your gut.

CHAPTER 4

Creating Mental Clarity

Stop worrying about what tomorrow may bring. Focus on what you can control. Stay positive. Enjoy today.

–Karen Salmansohn

I used to be a big people pleaser.

I would spend hours wondering what people thought of me. Every time after an interaction, making a presentation, or posting on social media, I would go into overthinking mode.

I would make up scenarios in my head. *What should I have said? What should I not have said? Was I supposed to act that way? Did they expect me to laugh at their jokes? What did they think?*

The thoughts would continue. Sometimes, it felt as if the thoughts would never stop. If someone told me something negative, I would look too much into it and waste time questioning what they meant by saying that.

To say that it bothered me would be a massive understatement. I would imagine different interactions with that person. I would imagine myself saying things differently or behaving in a way to get their approval.

I was so desperate to get others to like me that I was willing to change myself for their nod of agreement. I even abused alcohol to make myself more talkative and overcome my social anxiety. Drinking alcohol just made everything worse.

Eventually, I learned the hard way that you're never going to please everyone. It's just not possible. Because every time I tried to please others, I lost a bit of who I was. I lost the ability to trust myself and my gut feelings. Perhaps most importantly, I moved away from who I wanted to be.

It was a difficult journey, but I learned that if others want to think negatively about me, a presentation I gave, or a social media post I made, then I let them.

What others think of me is just not important. The only thing that really matters is what I think of myself, how I see myself, and what I can do to get myself closer to reaching my goals.

The same goes for you and your life. Does it matter what someone who brings no real value to your life thinks of you? Does it matter if people don't like your social media posts? Will it change your life if they don't approve of your choices?

I hope that by the end of this chapter, your answer to all three of these questions will be a big *no*.

The Power of Meditation and Mindfulness

Being more mindful in my daily life made a big difference in helping me overcome my people pleasing. I'm sure you've heard the word "mindfulness" many times before. You may even have already decided that it's not for you.

Many people are under a complete misconception of what mindfulness means. While sure, you can use your mindful times to meditate (and I highly recommend that you do), it's not just about sitting in a lotus position while breathing in and out.

You see, even though meditation is traditionally a spiritual practice, anyone can do it. You don't need to have a specific set of beliefs to meditate.

Meditation is also only one of many mindful practices you can add to your routine to bring an end to your overthinking. Before we get into that, let's first discuss what mindfulness is.

I'm going to keep this very simple: Mindfulness is basically a mental reset button. It's a way of forcing your mind to get quiet. It's about getting in touch with reality, not allowing your mind to be filled with regrets over past decisions or stressing over something that might never happen.

Think about a time you were obsessing over a conversation, stressing about a decision you had to make, or replaying scenarios over and over in your head. While your mind is racing, you're stuck. You can't break free from that cycle.

That's where mindfulness comes in. That is where you can press the reset button on your thoughts.

You see, being mindful makes you aware of what's going on inside your head without getting caught up in it. It's about observing your thoughts without judgment.

It's almost like taking a moment to watch your life from an outsider's perspective: You're standing on the sidewalk of a busy street (your life), watching the cars (your thoughts) race past. You can step into the street to stop a car, or you can simply watch until they've all passed.

This is what mindfulness can bring. It gives you:

- **Mental clarity:** You can stop overthinking a problem or situation because you've accepted your thoughts and are focused on what's happening in front of you.

- **Fewer emotional reactions:** Mindfulness helps you to pause, recognize your emotions, and then calm down before you respond.

- **Improved decision-making:** When you understand your thoughts and reduce your emotional reactions, you'll have the mental clarity to make better choices.

- **Reduced stress and anxiety:** When you're making better decisions and feel calmer in your present moment, your stress and anxiety levels will go down.

Before we go any further, I want you to keep in mind that mindfulness isn't a magic fix. You can't practice it once and believe you'll be cured of overthinking forever.

Instead, it's a practice that builds over time. It's something you need to do consistently. The more you practice, the better you get at calming your mind, especially when your overthinking wants to take over.

The best part? You start to see overthinking for what it is: a mental habit (as we discussed in the previous chapter), not a necessity.

Let's say you're preparing for a big meeting. Typically, you'd overthink every detail: obsessing over how you'll present the information, thinking about the "what-ifs," and maybe even losing sleep.

With mindfulness, you won't get wrapped up in your racing thoughts. Instead, you'll pause. You'll notice your thoughts without judgment. You'll take a few deep breaths, focus on your body, and bring your attention to the present. You may even visualize the meeting going well and remind yourself that you're ready.

By doing this, you're creating space between the trigger (stress about the meeting) and your response (overthinking). Do this regularly, and it can become second nature.

Now, before you allow your mind to spiral, wondering where you'll find time in your busy schedule, I have good news for you: You don't need to spend hours being mindful to see results. Even just five minutes of mindful breathing every day can help you become more aware of your thoughts and feelings.

You also don't have to sit still to practice mindfulness. If you're not the type to meditate, try adding other mindful activities to your day, like walking, running, or even weightlifting.

For example, while you're running, focus on every movement you make: the sound of your feet bouncing off the ground, the heavy sounds of your breathing, and the wind blowing over your sweaty skin. This will help to keep your thoughts in check.

You can also take multiple quick mindful pauses during the day. When you're stuck in traffic, before a big meeting, or even while having lunch, take a few seconds to close your eyes, take a deep breath, and notice how you're feeling.

While we'll discuss a few grounding techniques later in this chapter, I want you to quickly try this one: The 5-4-3-2-1 grounding technique.

This is a technique you can use at any time and in any situation where you find your mind starts to spiral. Here's how to do it:

- Identify 5 things you see.

- Acknowledge 4 things you feel.

- Note 3 things you hear.

- Recognize 2 things you smell.

- Name 1 thing you taste.

Because this technique uses your senses, it's quick to help you focus on what's going on around you, clearing your mind and reducing your anxiety in the process (Smith, 2018).

How Social Media Fuels Overthinking

I'm sure you've been there. You want to put something on social media, but instead of writing it and hitting the "post" button, you pause. You wait.

You overthink: *What will people think? Am I clear enough? Will they think I'm silly? What if they don't get me? What if I don't get any likes? Did I make a spelling mistake? Is my grammar correct? Do I look weird in that picture?*

The list of questions you might ask yourself goes on and on.

Or, perhaps your experience is different. Maybe looking at the posts of others results in your mind taking you all over the place. *Look how happy they look. Why can't I be that happy? Why can't I have perfectly white teeth? Why can't I be that successful? Where have I gone wrong? Is it too late for me to be successful? Why can't I ever be good enough?*

That's just the thing about social media. It's a double-edged sword.

Yes, social media is an amazing tool to keep you connected to loved ones and in touch with news from around the world. But spending too much time on these sites can also cause mental clutter and fuel your overthinking.

Let's look at some of the different ways in which social media can cause your mind to spiral:

- **Unrealistic comparisons:** Posts on social media are like a highlight reel of someone's life. It never shows you the full picture. People tend to post their best moments: luxury vacations, new cars, a perfect dinner, or a filtered selfie. The messy, behind-the-scenes stuff that makes up real life isn't shown. Comparing your complete life to someone else's filtered highlights creates a false sense of inadequacy.

- **FOMO (fear of missing out):** You've probably had that moment where you see a post about friends spending time together without inviting you. That sting you feel is the manifestation of FOMO. You start wondering: *Why wasn't I invited? Is there something wrong with me?*

- **Perfectionism in your posts:** Overthinking your posts can waste a lot of time and put a lot of pressure on yourself. You're editing, checking grammar, second-guessing yourself, wondering what you can change to get the maximum likes. You also analyze the feedback, wondering why someone didn't comment. This can make you even more nervous to post in the future.

- **Constant information overload:** With the constant flow of information—news, opinions, and education content—your brain is always in alert mode. You scroll through headlines, read too many opinions, and let every piece of new information into your brain. Then, you overthink it all. *What if that news story impacts my job? What if I miss out on an opportunity? What if the next big trend is something I need to know about right now?* It's like your brain is always working overtime.

Unsubscribing From Drama and Mental Clutter

If social media and digital distractions fuel your overthinking, it might be time to hit the unsubscribe button. And no, I'm not suggesting you delete all your accounts and go completely offline. There are ways to manage this without losing contact with your friends and family.

Let's look at a few changes you can make:

- **Limit your screen time:** Many apps can help you track the amount of time you spend on social media. You can also limit your scrolling to a few minutes over lunchtime only.

- **Unfollow accounts that trigger you:** Think about the accounts or people that make you feel bad about yourself, jealous, or even stressed. If you don't want to unfollow them entirely, you can mute their posts. Out of sight, out of mind.

- **Stop overanalyzing your own posts:** Before you post, ask yourself, *Why am I sharing this?* If it's to connect, go ahead. If it's because you feel like you have to or desperately want to get likes, take a step back. Reconsider if it's worth the mental effort you're going to put into it.

- **Focus on real connections:** While social media keeps you in contact with people from around the world, it should never replace face-to-face connections. Instead of scrolling, why not call a friend or plan a real get-together?

- **Reduce information overload:** It's easy to get lost in the information when you're mindlessly scrolling through social media sites. Instead, choose a few reliable sources only.

The digital age brings many benefits but also many distractions, which can fuel your overthinking. By being mindful of your use of social media and unsubscribing from the drama, you can take back control and start quieting the noise.

Learn to Listen to Your Gut

I'm sure you've heard people referring to their gut feelings when making decisions. Or perhaps someone has told you to trust your gut.

You might have ignored this advice and continued overthinking, believing you can only make a sound decision if you carefully look at the pros and cons, consider every possible worst-case scenario, or work through all the potential "what-ifs."

But here's the thing: Trusting your gut doesn't mean you should ignore all sense of logic. It's about listening to that inner voice that lets you know when something feels right or off.

Let's say you're out with friends, and someone suggests doing something risky, like driving somewhere after having a few too many drinks. Everyone else is in, but even though they say they are good to drive, your gut is telling you to order an Uber to take you home. Instead of overthinking what they might think of you or having FOMO, you trust that your instinct will keep you out of trouble.

Or, maybe you're about to buy a new car. You find a vehicle that seems decent and is in your price range. Everyone encourages you to go ahead with the purchase, but your gut tells you to hold off. A few weeks later, you find an even better deal.

Unfortunately, when you have to make a decision, you don't have the luxury of hindsight to know the best option. There may also be times when you're so driven by fear that you don't know what your gut is trying to tell you.

Let's say you get an exciting job offer. The salary is good, and it seems as if your work-life balance will improve if you take the job. Yet, something tells you to stay put at your current job.

Was this fear of failing? Or was it your gut feeling warning you? How do you tell the difference between gut-based feelings and fear-based thoughts?

This can be tricky. Both can trigger strong emotions and may feel similar in the moment. But there are key differences.

Let's first look at intuition, your gut feeling. This isn't something you analyze or rationalize. It's a deep, almost automatic sense of a situation, person, or decision. It's about instinctively applying your memories of past experiences and mixing them with your general awareness and knowledge.

When listening to your gut, it almost feels like an energy pulling you in a certain way. You'll feel calm and confident in your decisions. You know you're making the right choice, even if you don't know why you feel this way.

Fear is different. It's usually driven by anxiety, and your decisions are based on avoiding something bad or unpleasant. It often feels like a frantic energy pushing you back, causing you to feel tense and less confident.

How to Listen to Your Intuition

So, how do you do it? How do you know when your intuition is helping you to make decisions? How do you separate your gut feeling from fear-based thoughts? Here's a simple exercise that can help you:

- Write down a question about a life decision you're struggling with. For example, "Is now the right time to look for a new career opportunity?" or "Should I take on more responsibilities at work?"

- Underneath this question, write the two words "yes" and "no." Just that.

- Leave the paper for a few minutes. Do something to take your attention off this question. Then, once your mind feels free, come back to it.

- Without thinking about it, circle either "yes" or "no." Try to do it within two to three seconds.

- Take a few moments to pay attention to how you feel afterward, both physically and emotionally. Feeling calm and confident is a sign that you've listened to your gut.

Ground Your Racing Mind

A clear mind. That is key in stopping your overthinking for good. You need to be free from mental clutter and chaos to listen to your gut, reframe negative thoughts, and make quick decisions.

Unfortunately, it's easy to say you should have mental clarity, but when your thoughts are racing all over the place, it can be really difficult to reduce the noise. I mean, imagine sitting in a meeting where you're under pressure to make an important decision. Your heart is pounding so hard and your breathing is so heavy that you can't think clearly.

Luckily, there's a simple yet powerful solution: grounding.

This technique helps you to be more mindful and focused on the present moment rather than what could go wrong. It's a quick mental reset that snaps you out of your overthinking cycle and brings you back to reality.

The best thing about grounding? You can do it anywhere and anytime. Whether you're stuck in traffic, standing in line at the grocery store, stressing during a meeting, or relaxing at home, it gives you a moment to pause and reset.

Let's look at a few grounding techniques you can try.

Reset Phrases

Reset phrases are short, simple phrases you can use to stop your racing thoughts. They are quick reminders to help you refocus.

1. Choose a phrase that resonates with you and makes you feel calm. For example, "I am here and in control" or "One step at a time."

2. When you notice that you're overthinking, say the phrase, either silently in your head or out loud if you can.

3. Repeat it as many times as you need to. While you're doing this, focus only on the words and their meaning. You can even close your eyes to give your body and mind a break.

4. After a few repetitions, notice your thoughts slowing down. Continue doing this until you feel calm and in control.

Tactile Anchors

When you use tactile anchors, you focus on physical sensations to bring you back to the present.

1. Hold a physical object in your hand. It could be anything from a stress ball, a smooth stone, a pencil, or even a piece of clothing.

2. Close your eyes and pay attention only to how it feels. Notice the texture, temperature, and weight. Try to feel every detail.

3. Let your mind stay on this sensation for a few moments until you find your mind is clearer.

Mental Interruption

This technique is excellent in disrupting the endless loop of overthinking. Mental interruption is like flipping a switch to reset your brain.

1. When you catch yourself overthinking, say something like "Stop!" or "Take a break" out loud or in your head. This is the first mental interruption.

2. Then, immediately do something else. It can be as simple as looking in the other direction or deliberately listening to sounds around you.

3. Your third mental interruption is to do something physical. Try standing up, stretching, or taking a quick walk around the room.

The key is to interrupt your thoughts long enough to break the cycle of overthinking, giving your mind a few moments to reset.

Mindful Observation

Mindful observation is about focusing on your surroundings rather than your thoughts. It's paying attention to the details you may otherwise overlook.

1. Find a place where you can sit quietly and comfortably. If you can't find a quiet place, close your eyes to drown out the external noise.

2. Pick something in your environment. It could be a tree outside, an object in the room, or even the sound of a car driving down the street.

3. Pay only attention to that object or sound. Look at the details: its shape, color, texture, and size. If you're focusing on a sound, listen to the pitch of the sound or changes in the noise. Pretend like you're seeing or hearing it for the first time.

4. Continue focusing on it for a few minutes. This helps refocus your mind and calm your overactive thoughts.

10-Minute Exercise: Visualize Calm

Visualization is another grounding technique that can be very effective in stopping overthinking. When you visualize yourself handling one of your overthinking triggers, you train your mind to respond calmly.

1. **Find a quiet space:** Start by finding a comfortable place where you won't be disturbed. Sit or lie down in a relaxed position. If you're at work, you can even do this during a quick bathroom break.

2. **Focus on your breathing:** Close your eyes. Inhale deeply through your nose for a count of four, hold your breath for a count of four, and exhale slowly through your mouth for a count of four. Repeat this a few times until you feel calm.

3. **Think of an overthinking trigger:** Don't dive too deep into the emotions or the specifics—just recognize the general trigger.

4. **Visualize the trigger happening:** Imagine that you are in that very situation now, where the overthinking would typically start. What's happening around you? How do you feel physically? What's going through your mind?

5. **Shift to calmness:** Now, picture yourself handling this situation calmly. Feel how the tension in your body goes away as you continue to take slow, deep breaths.

6. **Do a grounding technique:** As you visualize this moment, apply one of the grounding techniques discussed above. Picture yourself remaining calm throughout this exercise.

7. **See yourself responding:** Now, see yourself responding to this situation or trigger with confidence and a calm mind.

8. **Reinforce the positive outcome:** Visualize feeling good about yourself and in control of the situation.

9. **End with an affirmation:** Before finishing the exercise, say a positive affirmation to yourself. This could be something like: *I have the power to stay calm and clear, no matter the situation.*

Chapter Summary

- Mindfulness is like a mental reset button that helps you stay in the present moment. It gives you mental clarity, reduces emotional responses and stress, and improves decision-making.

- Social media can fuel overthinking through unrealistic comparisons, wanting your posts to be perfect, and FOMO.

- Unsubscribing from mental clutter can help you gain peace of mind without completely going offline.

- Trusting your gut means listening to your intuition without overthinking every decision. When you listen to your gut, you'll feel calm and confident in your decisions.

***

As you rediscover your mental clarity and learn to listen to your gut without allowing your mind to spiral, you're getting ready to actively tackle your overthinking. Never allow this process to overwhelm you. Focus on taking one small action, or micro action, at a time, as we'll discuss in the next chapter.

CHAPTER 5

The 10-Minute Reset—The Micro Action That Breaks Overthinking

You don't have to see the whole staircase, just take the first step.

–Martin Luther King, Jr.

For many years, I believed I wasn't good at speaking.

As a child, I had to constantly repeat myself because I would mumble my words. I hated giving presentations because people would laugh at my pronunciation. I was also very shy, and talking to a group of people completely intimidated me.

I was ridiculed and bullied. I went to speech therapy for many years and was told I had a speech impediment. Every time I had to speak in front of others, my insecurities would come up.

During presentations, my heart was pounding, my hands were shaking, I was stuttering, and I forgot my words, making me look stupid.

The thought of everyone staring at me, judging me, laughing at me, felt suffocating. Even while attending college, I felt like that small boy again who got bullied.

The fear always felt so real. It wasn't just the idea of failing; it was the thought of everyone seeing me fail.

But I liked to feel in control. That need for control pushed me to not allow these insecurities to get the best of me. So, I took action. I started small by joining a fraternity and going to social events to talk to strangers.

I took on leadership roles to grow my confidence. I forced myself to communicate, did door-to-door sales, and eventually even joined Toastmasters to overcome that fear of public speaking. That voice in my head criticizing me for being a bad speaker became smaller and smaller.

I no longer feel that way. Now, I can go to any event and talk to anyone. As I've mentioned already, I even started my own youth motivational speaking business. I got paid to speak to people in different states and even other countries.

This change in mindset has made a massive difference. For the past 10+ years, I've been working with people in different capacities. In my latest role as customer success manager, I'm responsible for building client relationships. If it wasn't for this change in mindset, I would never be able to speak confidently.

Sure, sometimes those thoughts do creep in, and I blame certain failures for the way I speak. My accent will always be different compared to most people, and that's okay. The difference is that now, I don't allow those thoughts to change my actions.

Who would've thought a kid who got bullied for how he spoke and went to speech therapy now gets paid to run his mouth? It's amazing how life works out.

I've learned to accept myself with compassion. I've learned to take micro-actions whenever I feel overwhelmed. I use strategies to make quick decisions so my mind doesn't spiral out of control.

You may not have a specific insecurity that you're struggling with. Perhaps you're looking at improving a skill or are overthinking a big decision you have to make. Whatever the case is for you, you can do it. You can take action, one step at a time, to bring the change you desire.

More Action, Less Rumination

Take a moment to think about your overthinking. What do you do when your mind spirals? Do you freeze and stay in the same position? Is it easy to stop your racing thoughts while you're still? Do you procrastinate with no end in sight?

I don't know about you, but whenever I sit still for too long, my mind races a lot more than when I'm doing something. When I'm productive, I feel more in control of my thoughts. When I'm taking a step forward, regardless of how small, I feel like I'm getting somewhere.

I've found that taking action is one of the best ways to break free from overthinking. It's quite simple: When you're taking action, you focus on what you're doing, not your thoughts. You do something other than procrastinate in your thoughts.

Also, when you're taking action, you're lowering your anxiety, as you'll feel like you're making a difference in your life, not just sitting in self-pity and stress (Jennings & Kubala, 2023).

You see, nothing will ever change unless you do something about it. Your relationship with your partner won't improve unless you work out what problems you may have and find solutions together. Your performance at work won't improve unless you upskill yourself. You won't suddenly gain financial security unless you rework your budget to boost your savings.

You need to take that step. You need to do something. You need to be more productive, not just feel busy because of how much you're thinking. Instead of going over and over what might happen or what could go wrong, focus only on what's in front of you—right there, in the moment.

This is how action shifts your attention from feeling paralyzed by your overthinking to being productive and making good decisions. It's how you go from procrastinating to being productive.

Think of it like this: Overthinking is like being stuck in a mental traffic jam. All you do is sit, wait, worry about not getting anywhere, and hope that somehow, things will just work out. But, when you take action, even if it's something simple like sending an email or making a call, you're essentially putting the car in gear and driving. You're doing something productive.

That small act of movement gets you out of the mental traffic jam. It creates momentum in the right direction. It helps you stop overthinking and procrastination.

The Micro-Action Approach

I'll always remember that feeling: the doubt, the fear, and the uncertainty that comes with taking action, whether it was making a choice or following through with a decision. For way too long, I've allowed my overthinking to paralyze me. I was so stuck in my head that I couldn't do anything.

When I had to take action, whether it was to physically do something or make a decision, I would go into my endless loop of worrying if I was making the right decision, how people would perceive me, how many mistakes I'd make, or what would happen if I didn't do it perfectly. I was questioning every step. I was completely overwhelmed.

That was, until I heard about the micro-action approach.

That taught me the importance of starting small. Taking one step at a time. Focusing on the very next thing I had to do, not the task as a whole. You don't focus on how much you've procrastinated or how much you're stuck in your thoughts. You only focus on your next step.

This approach is about taking small, manageable steps, or micro-actions, that will result in fast actions directly tied to the problem at hand.

Because you aren't working on the entire task or project as a whole, each small step doesn't have to be perfect. It just needs to get done, which massively helped my perfectionistic side.

And, since no one else saw each little step I took, I didn't have to worry about pleasing anyone. I just had to work on getting it done. One foot in front of the other.

Now, you may wonder how it looks in reality. Let's say you're thinking about starting a business. It can be extremely stressful. You need to draft a business plan, possibly secure investors, maybe look for affordable premises, decide on a name, a slogan, and a logo, decide how your product fits in the market, do marketing, and so forth. It's a lot.

Thinking about everything that needs to be done can be overwhelming. So, why not break it down into smaller steps? For example, you can start by researching one or two competitors. Since you know exactly what you need to do, there's much less room for overthinking.

Once you're done, you move on to the next step. You might not feel like you're getting much done, but you are. You're building momentum. One small step leads to another. Before you know it, you've created something solid.

It's almost like building: You stack one brick on top of the other until you eventually have a wall.

Still not convinced? Let's look at another example, this time of a personal goal like wanting to improve your fitness. Since this goal isn't specific, you'll easily find yourself overthinking: *Should I join a gym? What type of exercises should I do? Do I need to take a supplement? What about a shake? What is actually in a shake? What if I injure myself? What if I join a gym but never go? How much money will I waste? Can I afford a gym membership? What should I eat? Do I eat before I work out or afterward? How will I know if I'm doing it right?*

I can go on and on. I've also been there more than once.

How can you break this down into a micro-action? Your first step could be something as simple as stretching for five minutes or taking a quick walk after work. It's nothing crazy, but it gets the ball rolling. It creates momentum. Soon enough, you'll find yourself ready to take on bigger challenges.

Micro-actions are also powerful when it comes to trusting your gut. Maybe you're unsure about taking a new job. Instead of overthinking the risks, why don't you reach out to someone already in the field or at the company to learn more? It's only one quick phone call, but it can make a massive difference.

That small step creates movement. And that movement helps validate your gut feeling, giving you confidence in your decisions. The more you act on those gut feelings with micro-actions, the stronger your trust in yourself will become, helping you break the cycle of doubt and overthinking for good.

Boost Your Decision-Making

Now, let's move to something I'm sure every overthinker struggles with: making decisions.

I'm sure you've been there: You're staring at your computer, trying to figure out whether to send that email about a suggestion for a new project to your boss. You've written it, reworded it, and deleted it three times, wondering if there's a better way to say things. You've even copied it to a few AI sites to see if it can be worded better. Eventually, you hope for the best and press send.

You're tired from the day, then it's the next choice: where to eat. You would've been happy with making a quick meal at home, but your partner wants to go out—and they want you to decide where to go. They want to be spoiled.

Again, the endless questions fill your mind. *Where do we go? What place would be good enough? Do I have enough money for a fancy dinner? What must I wear? What time must we leave? What time will we be home? Will I get to bed early enough? I'm so exhausted. What if I fall asleep at the dinner table?*

This choice might seem small and insignificant, but after a long day at work, you just want to relax and prepare for the next day. When you're in this frame of mind, even the most insignificant decisions can be overwhelming.

You see, overthinking can make everything feel like a high-stakes decision, even when it's not. It's exhausting: constantly weighing every possible outcome, fearing the wrong choice, and questioning if you've considered everything.

This is why every overthinker needs an arsenal of techniques to help them make quick decisions. Fast decision-making strategies help you cut through the mental noise and avoid getting caught in analysis paralysis. Here are a few of my favorites.

The Three-Second Rule

When faced with a decision, give yourself three seconds to make a choice. Just that, only three seconds for a quick decision. Trust your gut, as we discussed in the previous chapter, and act before your mind has time to spiral out of control. While this rule is best used for small decisions that won't have a big impact on your life, you can even use it for bigger ones as well, like deciding whether to take that job offer.

The Decision Filter

The decision filter is almost like a mental checklist. When you have to make a decision, ask yourself questions like, *Will this choice help me reach my goal?* or *What will happen if I don't make this decision?* These types of questions act like a filter, helping you narrow down your options without overthinking all the details.

For example, if you're deciding whether to take on an extra project at work, use this filter to see if or how this additional project will help you reach your long-term goals. Does it support your career growth? Will it just add stress without really moving you forward? After answering these questions, you'll feel more confident in your decision, knowing you've focused on what matters most.

Delegate Your Decisions

There may be some decisions you can pass on to your partner, or if you own a business, you may give some of your staff members the authority to make certain decisions.

The thing is, as much as you want to be in control all the time, there may be people in your life who can help you make a choice. This will not only help to ease the pressure of making the decision that was on you and reduce your overthinking, but it will also build trust in your relationships.

Be Prepared

Not all decisions have to be made in a crunch moment. Sometimes, you can prepare your choices in advance. This will help reduce the pressure you would otherwise feel when you have to make them.

For example, if you overthink what you should wear in the mornings, why not set out your clothes the night before when you're feeling more relaxed? This will help you start the day feeling fresh and prepared.

Another example can be creating your goals for the week on a Sunday. This would help you know exactly what needs to be done, reducing the mental chaos you might have when you aren't sure of what your next step should be.

Small Decisions Firsts

Starting with small decisions is an excellent way to build momentum. Getting these minor choices out of the way will help you feel like you can get things done. This will then push you to do even more.

Let's say you have an email to respond to. There's no rush to reply immediately, so you could let it sit for a few hours. But it will always be in the back of your mind, which can make it difficult to focus on more important tasks. If you take care of it immediately, you free your mind.

The more you do this and create a habit of making smaller decisions first, the less you'll procrastinate on other tasks.

The Five-Year Test

When faced with a tough decision, ask yourself: *Will this matter in five years?* If the answer is no, is it worth stressing over? Will it matter whether you don't get it done perfectly?

Let's say you have an important event you need to attend. Suddenly, you feel paralyzed by the choice of what to wear. *Do I dress formally? What if everyone else is in casual clothes? What will they think of me?*

Now, ask yourself if it will matter in five years. Will your outfit make any actual difference? Or are you wasting time with your indecision?

While some decisions will have a lasting impact on your life, most won't.

Reverse Engineering the Decision

Imagine you've already made your decision. Everything has worked out quite well. Now, think backward. Retrace your steps. What did you do to get there? What decisions did you have to make along the way? Using this strategy helps you visualize yourself achieving success, which builds your confidence in making a decision.

For example, if you're wondering if you should take on a leadership role at work, imagine that you've already accepted the role. It's been going well. You've made the right choice. Now, work out how you got there.

The Ask-a-Friend Method

Sometimes, all you need is a sounding board. You know, someone to talk to. Someone you trust to give you advice. Someone with a fresh set of eyes who isn't emotionally involved can help you decide. For example, if you're considering moving to a new town, talking to someone close to you may help you think of aspects you may have overlooked.

It can even be that it's not their input that helps you make a choice, but hearing yourself talk about the decision you need to make that gives you a different perspective.

10-Minute Exercise: Actions to Disrupt Overthinking

Let's look at a few micro-actions you can do in only 10 minutes to interrupt your overthinking and clear your mind. Pick one of these actions daily:

- **Write down your thoughts:** Take 10 minutes to get your thoughts out of your head and onto a piece of paper or the notepad on your phone. This can be journaling, doing a brain dump, or even listing your worries.

- **Organize your space:** When your physical spaces are chaotic or full of clutter, you'll struggle to organize your thoughts. Take 10 minutes to tidy up your desk or home. When your environment feels organized, your mind will follow.

- **Practice deep breathing:** When your mind is spiraling, your body usually tenses up. This makes it harder to think clearly. Try to relax with 10 minutes of deep breathing or even a short meditation session.

- **Write down one small decision you can make:** Pick a small, insignificant decision you can make in the next 10 minutes. This can be choosing what to have for dinner or responding to a text message.

- **Listen to music or a podcast:** Take 10 minutes to listen to a song or podcast that distracts you from your worries. This can also help to lift your overall mood.

- **Reconnect with someone:** Having a quick conversation with a friend or family member can stop your overthinking.

- **Work toward a goal:** Take 10 minutes to work on a goal you have. This can be completing a short goal or taking the next step toward a long-term goal.

- **Do something physical:** Exercise isn't just good for your physical body but can help you clear your mind as well. Take

10 minutes to do something physical, whether it's going for a walk, a jog, a gym session, or even just some yoga stretches.

Chapter Summary

- Overthinking happens more when you're not doing anything. When you're busy or productive, your focus shifts from worrying to doing. It gives you something to do.

- The micro-action approach is about breaking down tasks into small, manageable steps that help you move forward. Because you're taking small steps, you don't have to get it done perfectly.

- Many overthinkers struggle with making decisions because they overanalyze every possible outcome. This can not only make you feel exhausted but also stops you from doing anything.

- Techniques to cut through analysis paralysis include the three-second rule, the decision filter, delegating your decisions, being prepared, making small decisions first, the five-year test, reverse engineering your decision, and asking a friend.

***

Overthinking can show up in all areas of your life. After a long day of overanalyzing at work, the last thing you probably want when you step into your home is to feel paralyzed in your relationship or friendships.

In the next chapter, we'll look at specific strategies you can use to avoid draining your mental energy in these areas of your life.

CHAPTER 6

Overcoming Overthinking in Work, Relationships, and Daily Life

People become attached to their burdens sometimes more than the burdens are attached to them.

–George Bernard Shaw

Do you enjoy your career? Are you excited about getting up each morning to spend the majority of your day at work? Do you feel satisfied with your work performance? Or do you overthink it?

Perhaps you feel like you constantly have to prove yourself. Maybe you struggle to deal with the pressure to succeed. You may even question your entire career path altogether, from the type of work you do to whether you have the skills to do the job.

Then, there is the balancing act of trying to fit everything into your life. You want to do your best at work. You want to be there for the people in your life. You want to make time for yourself. And you want to do all of this without failing. It's tough.

I used to overthink that I hated my job and wasn't going to find success in my career. The only type of work I've had before was working at a family startup, where I had a lot of different responsibilities. I became the jack of all trades, master of none.

I wanted more. I saw others opening businesses, so I also tried. I saw others starting social media channels, so I tried. I always tried to measure up to others' standards. And, way too often, I failed.

I tried to venture into different careers, often the ones others would tell me I'd be good at. But the only type of jobs I could get were sales jobs. One of these was in the logistics field. I was overworked, underpaid, undervalued, burnt out, and the company didn't have good benefits or paid time off. That job destroyed my confidence.

Every day, I felt like I wasn't good enough. Like I didn't have any real skills. And I didn't enjoy working in sales. I felt trapped, not just in my job but also in my overthinking mind.

To bring structure to my thoughts, I started to look at my strengths and what I enjoyed doing. This change in mindset helped me break free from the negatives. Now, I focus on the positives: I loved speaking that didn't involve cold sales. I was good at building relationships with customers. I often got complimented on how I explain technology.

I used these strengths as a starting point to research new career opportunities and stumbled across the career path of a customer success manager. Based on my strengths, I thought this was a perfect fit. I committed to taking small daily actions to get me closer to this type of job: fixing my résumé, practicing interview questions, applying for jobs, and networking with others in this field.

A year and a half later, I landed a position as a customer success manager at a growing tech company. I love it there; I am valued, and I am doing well in my job.

Don't ever underestimate the power of doing what feels right for you, not what feels right for others. It doesn't matter if you second-guess yourself in your career choices, relationships, or other aspects of life. If you do what feels right for you, you'll feel more motivated to reach your goals. You'll feel happier, and your mind will be calmer.

The Curse of Second-Guessing

Let's start by looking at second-guessing yourself. We've all done that. We spend so much time considering every "what if" or "I should've" scenario that doesn't just slow you down; it drains your mental energy. Replaying every decision or situation will lead to burnout. Trust me, I've been there.

It almost feels like you're driving with your car's parking brake still slightly engaged. You're pressing down hard on the accelerator, but the car just doesn't get up to speed. You're just not moving forward. The longer you drive like this, the more damage you can cause to your car's entire brake system.

The same goes for second-guessing. The more you doubt yourself, the less you accomplish, and the more you damage your mental clarity.

Let's look at a few techniques you can use in all aspects of your life—work, relationships, personal growth, and even your health—to end your second-guessing.

Create a "Doubt Jar"

This technique might sound a little unusual, but trust me; it works. Every time you notice that you're second-guessing, write about your doubt on a piece of paper, and put it in the jar. At the end of the month (or once your jar is full), look at all the doubts you've had. You might be surprised how many times you were doubting things that weren't important or made no real difference in your life. This will also help you to identify triggers and patterns in your overthinking.

"Fake It Until You Believe It" Body Language

You likely don't feel confident when your mind is filled with doubts. Why not fake it until you believe it? Here's how it works: When you feel self-doubt taking over, adjust your posture and body language. Stand tall, push your shoulders back, uncross your arms and legs, and lift your chin. These subtle tweaks in your posture can make a massive difference in how you feel about yourself. The better you feel, the more confident you'll be, and the less you'll second-guess yourself.

Go on a Doubt Diet

Much like how you can reduce unhealthy foods for better physical health, "doubt dieting" is about reducing your doubts. It's quite simple: Decide on how many doubts you'll let yourself have daily. Then, create a log where you note every time you catch yourself second-guessing a decision. Once you've reached your limit, you're done doubting for the day.

Yes, I know this may sound ridiculous, but it's surprisingly helpful in freeing up your mind.

After a few weeks, you can reduce your number of allowed doubts in a day until you're only left with one or two daily.

Find a "Doubt Buddy"

Find someone you trust who's also struggling with second-guessing, and form a "doubt buddy" system. When one of you starts spiraling with doubt, have a check-in. This can be a face-to-face conversation or even a quick phone call. Instead of just venting during this time, challenge each other to find solutions and share perspectives you might not have considered. Remind one another that it's natural and normal to doubt but you should never allow your doubts to stop you from moving forward.

Reframe Second-Guessing as Exploring

Change how you see your second-guessing. Instead of seeing it as a weakness keeping you back, reframe it as a time for exploring. If you're unsure about a decision you need to make, tell yourself that you're simply exploring options. This way, you're approaching it as curiosity rather than fear of making the wrong choice. Because of this change in mindset, you're less likely to get stuck in a loop of second-guessing.

Commit to a "No Second-Guessing Day"

Choose one day a week (or month if you're starting) where you commit to not second-guessing any decision you have to make. It doesn't matter if this is while you're at work or home; you commit to choosing without questioning yourself. Doing this will almost be like a mental cleanse, which can help boost your confidence and teach you how good you'll feel if you make quick decisions.

Practice "Anti-Perfectionism"

Instead of wanting every decision to be perfect, intentionally do something you know from the start won't be perfect. The first few times doing this might be scary, but it's a great way of training your mind that every decision doesn't have to be flawless. You are allowed to make mistakes and should embrace these mistakes as opportunities to learn and be creative.

Overanalyzing Conversations and Social Interactions

You know that feeling: You leave a work meeting or a get-together with friends, and suddenly, you're replaying the entire interaction in your mind, obsessing over every word that was said. *Why did I say that? I should've said something else. I sounded like an idiot!*

Or maybe you're wondering about other people's behavior: *What did they mean when they said that?* Or you tell yourself, *I was the most awkward person there*, or *I shared way too much.* You might even worry that you hurt someone's feelings without realizing it.

You get stuck questioning everything, even the most innocent interactions. To make it worse, you remember only the negative aspects of your interactions. It's as if nothing positive happened.

This is called post-event rumination. It feeds any anxieties or worries you may have about interacting with others and makes you feel like you're stuck in your head.

Apart from being a potential sign of social anxiety and general anxiety, overthinking your interactions can also be a sign of low self-esteem (Sims, n.d.). It can be that you don't feel comfortable or safe around others or you fear rejection and disappointing others.

Low self-esteem can show up in different ways. You may lack confidence in certain areas, like your career or relationships. Perhaps you feel self-assured about what you do but struggle to accept recognition for your hard work or effort.

If you're like me, your lack of self-esteem can also come from people-pleasing. You may think that only if you get their approval can you feel good about yourself.

Past traumas, such as being bullied or heavily criticized, can also affect your self-esteem. These experiences create beliefs about not being "good enough" or "lovable," and your brain naturally tries to protect you by staying hyper-alert, always looking for signs of potential rejection.

The result? You start to feel like you're always being judged, even when you aren't. It's a way for you to cope and protect yourself. Unfortunately, doing this only increases your anxiety, making it even more difficult to connect with others.

The good news is that just like you can stop overthinking in all other areas of your life, you can also put an end to overanalyzing your social interactions.

The middle steps—how you evaluate yourself and how you ruminate—are where the real change happens. Here are a few of my favorite techniques to use.

Create a Distraction Ritual After Social Events

Instead of analyzing what went wrong or what could've been better after a social interaction, distract yourself on purpose. It could be something simple, like having a quick workout, doing a hobby or activity you enjoy, or listening to a podcast that has nothing to do with the event. This helps to break the cycle of obsessing over what you said, what they might've thought, what they might've meant, or any "what-ifs" your mind might come up with.

The Five-Minute Rule

Once you get home after a social event, set a timer for five minutes. This is the only time you're allowed to replay the conversations in your head. No more than five minutes. Try to counter every negative aspect of the interaction with something that went well. If you can't think of any positives, come up with ideas of how you'd like to behave differently the next time you're in a similar situation. When the timer goes off, tell yourself that you're done thinking about it and deliberately move on.

Visualize the Next Step

If you struggle to pinpoint any positives of your interactions or don't know what you can do to improve, it can be helpful to visualize what happens next. Take a few minutes (not more than 10) to think about your next step. This doesn't necessarily have to be related to your social life. It can also be something mundane, like going home, making dinner, or getting back to your routine. It doesn't matter what you visualize. The value lies in shifting your brain to change the focus from replaying past moments to looking ahead.

Play the Other Side

If you're worried about saying something awkward in a conversation, try a trick I call "playing the other side." All this means is to switch your perspective and imagine that someone else told you what you just said. How would you have interpreted it? Would you be upset if someone said that to you? Is what happened worth increasing your anxiety by overthinking about it? In most cases, you'd likely realize it wasn't a big deal.

Track Your Social Wins

Start a "social wins" journal or a simple note on your phone where you record every positive social interaction or small victory you had during a discussion. It could be as simple as a good joke you told, a meaningful conversation, or a positive comment someone made to you. The next time your mind starts to spiral into the typical thoughts of *What did I say wrong?* or *They probably think I'm weird*, pull up your list of wins. This will help you realize that not all of your interactions are as bad as you might've thought they'd be.

Set Boundaries to Save Your Energy

In many cases, the cause of your social anxiety or overthinking might not be due to something you've said or done. It can also be a result of how other people behave. Since you can't control the behaviors of others, what can you do to reduce the impact this has on you?

The answer is simple: You need to set boundaries with the people who drain your energy.

Take a moment to picture yourself spending your time and energy exactly how you want to. What if I tell you that boundaries can do exactly that?

They're the invisible lines that help you manage how much of yourself you're willing to give to others and what you're willing to accept back from them. In everyday life, boundaries can show up in all sorts of ways, from saying no to something you don't want to do or have time for to how you handle interruptions during family time.

Take this example: You've had a long week at work, and all you want is a quiet night at home. A friend calls and asks if you want to grab a drink. You don't want to let them down, but you know you're already running on empty.

A healthy boundary here is recognizing your need for rest and saying, "I'd love to hang out, but I need some downtime tonight." This boundary isn't about being rude or selfish; it's about respecting your needs and putting yourself first.

Or, picture yourself at the office. You already feel like you have too much on your plate. Suddenly, your boss asks you to take on one more urgent task. You can feel the stress building up while your mind starts to spiral.

Instead of giving in to the pressure and fear of disappointing your boss, a healthy boundary would be to calmly explain your current workload and then ask your boss what they'd like you to do. You could say something like: "I'm already handling a few critical tasks with tight deadlines. How can we prioritize these tasks so I can fit in the new task? Or would it be possible to delegate this to someone else?"

By setting this boundary, you're showing your boss you're willing to do it, so your fear of disappointing them is no longer valid. But you're also telling them you're already under pressure and put the ball back in their court to change things around. You're protecting your time while also setting expectations for what you can realistically manage. You're protecting your mind from situations in which it would spiral out of control.

Unfortunately, as much as you may understand the need for boundaries, your anxiety can make this tricky.

Your people-pleasing tendencies may be that voice in the back of your head suggesting that you need to say yes to every request. Or wondering what people will think of you if you don't put the needs of others first. You may even sacrifice your peace of mind to avoid the anxiety that can come with conflict.

While the thought of setting boundaries can lead to anxiety, not setting boundaries can also make you more anxious. It's a vicious cycle.

The good news is that only the first few boundaries will be challenging to set. The more you do it, the easier it will get. The more healthy boundaries you set, the more your anxiety will decrease.

You see, boundaries aren't there to control others. It's not about telling others what they can and can't do. It's about telling people what you want and don't want. It's like putting a fence around you, where you can decide who and what you want to open the gate for.

Let's break it down into some easy steps for setting boundaries:

- **Know what you want:** You can't set boundaries if you don't know what you want and need. When you know exactly what your priorities are, it's easier to have a calm mind. Take a moment and ask yourself, *What's draining me right now? What would I rather want? What do I need most?*

- **Communicate clearly:** Once you know what you need, communicate it. You need to be clear without over-explaining or apologizing for setting these boundaries. Just say it as straightforward as you can without overthinking it or trying to justify it.

- **Start small:** If setting boundaries feels like a huge step, start small. Maybe it's setting a limit on how many times a week you'll join happy hour with coworkers. telling a friend that you only have 30 minutes for a catch-up because you have other things to take care of as well.

- **Be consistent:** Once you've set a boundary, stick to it. For example, if you've told a friend you're not available for late-night phone calls during the week, don't slip back into old habits because you feel bad.

- **Don't fear a reaction:** Most people will respect your boundaries once you set them. And if they don't? Well, that's on them, not you. You're just taking care of yourself. Let's say a family member asks for help with something last-minute, and you've already planned your evening to recharge. A boundary here might be telling them something like, "I can't do it tonight, but I'm free this weekend."

- **Check in regularly:** Set aside time every few weeks to check in with yourself. Are you still comfortable with the boundaries you've set? Are there areas where you've let things slide? For example, if you notice that your weekends are always packed with commitments you didn't plan for, a new boundary could be something like: *Weekends are for family and rest. I'll say no to any non-essential plans.*

Always remember that boundaries aren't about saying no. They're about saying yes to what matters, like your time, energy, and mental clarity.

10-Minute Exercise: Address Your Difficult Thoughts

Let's do a quick exercise to help you identify the areas of your life where overthinking drains your energy the most. This will help you realize where you need to put boundaries and what small actions you can take to protect your energy.

Step 1: Identify the Areas of Your Life Affected by Overthinking

Think about the parts of your life most affected by overthinking. These might be situations that cause you stress, anxiety, or even procrastination, and can include:

- **Work:** Do you hesitate to make decisions at work because you fear making a mistake? Maybe you avoid taking risks or going for big opportunities because you're not sure if you're ready.

- **Relationships and social situations:** Do you often analyze what people say and do? Do you second-guess how someone might feel after a conversation?

- **Health:** Do you struggle to improve your lifestyle because you fear not doing it right? Do you overthink going to the doctor for a general checkup?

- **Personal growth:** Are you stuck in "what ifs" or "I should've" thinking? Maybe you regret not taking action on something in the past, and it's stopping you from moving forward now.

Step 2: Write Down the Specific Thoughts You Have in These Areas

For each area you identified, make a list of the types of thoughts you have most often. Be as specific as possible.

Work

- *What if I mess up the presentation?*
- *What if I'm not good enough?*
- *How will it look if I fail?*

Relationships and Social Situations

- *Did I say something weird?*
- *What if I hurt their feelings by accident?*
- *What if I sound needy when I text them?*

Health

- *What if I don't do the workout correctly?*
- *What if I blow my diet by eating a candy bar?*

- *What if the doctor gives me bad news?*

Personal growth

- *What if it's too late for me now?*

- *I should've started this years ago.*

- *I'll never be good enough at this.*

Step 3: Develop Actionable Steps to Break the Cycle of Overthinking

Now that you have a better idea of how overthinking shows up in the different parts of your life, let's take action. For each area, come up with one step you can take to move forward.

- **Work:** Choose one small task you've been putting off and do it right away. It could be sending that email, starting the first draft of your presentation, or asking for feedback. Do it without second-guessing yourself.

- **Relationships and social situations:** If you're unsure about a conversation, send a quick follow-up message to clear any uncertainty. Do it immediately; if you wait too long, the other person might not remember the conversation that you're overanalyzing.

- **Health:** Set a small, manageable fitness goal, like exercising for five minutes every morning or going for a 10-minute walk after work. Commit to doing just that one thing every day.

- **Personal growth:** Break down a personal goal into its smallest component and focus on taking one small action today. It doesn't have to be perfect, just start.

Step 4: Reflect and Adjust

After taking your small action, reflect on how it made you feel. Did it help you move forward? Did it stop your overthinking? Keep taking these small steps. You're building momentum that will help you tackle bigger challenges without getting stuck in your thoughts.

Chapter Summary

- Overthinking can have a big impact on different parts of your life, including your work, relationships, and social interactions. It can cause you to second-guess even the most insignificant details.

- Overthinking social interactions is also called post-event rumination, where you focus only on negative aspects. This feeds social anxiety and general anxiety. It can also be a result of low self-esteem.

- Boundaries can help to protect your time, energy, and mental clarity. Fear of disappointing others or conflict can make it hard to set boundaries, but not having them can make you even more anxious.

- Boundaries protect your needs. They are about saying yes to your well-being, not just no to anything that will keep you from living your best life.

***

You've come a long way in stopping your overthinking for good. Take a minute to pat yourself on the back. Many people would've given up already, but you're still going strong. You're still motivated to create momentum and take back control of your life. In the next section, we'll look at steps you can take to make sure overthinking becomes (and stays) a thing of the past.

PART 3

Making Overthinking a Thing of the Past

CHAPTER 7

Taking Back Your Time, Energy, and Mental Bandwidth

Take time to deliberate, but when the time for action has arrived, stop thinking and go in.

–Napoleon Bonaparte

Have you ever had a goal so big that it scares you? Maybe it's opening your own business. Perhaps it's committing to your partner and starting a family. Or, maybe it's something simpler, like getting through a day without overthinking.

Instead of taking that first step to making it a reality, what is your most likely response? Paralysis? Freezing completely?

You've thought it through a thousand times, but somehow, the more you think, the more overwhelming it becomes. You get stuck in your head, imagining all the ways things could go wrong, all the mistakes you might make, and suddenly it feels like you're drowning in possibilities.

You want to take that step. You want to make it happen. But you remain motionless while your frustration levels boil over.

I've been there. One of my scariest goals was wanting to run a marathon. Even though the desire was there, I was paralyzed by my thoughts: *How will I find the time to train? What if I train and can't finish? How much pain will I be in?*

Luckily for me, a friend had the same dream. This friend wouldn't allow me to overthink too much. We decided to sign up and figure the rest out later.

Training for the marathon wasn't always easy, but I made sure that I trained at least three days a week. Sometimes, I would train at 8 p.m. on a Friday. Sometimes, I would be running by 5 a.m. on a weekend.

I'm not going to lie to you or pretend that it was easy or that I looked forward to training. Half the time, I was in deep pain at the end of a session. But, I was aware of my triggers to overthinking. I constantly reminded myself not to go down that path.

Six months later, I completed the Disney Marathon. I didn't quite make the time I wanted. In the past, I would've beaten myself up over being too slow. This time, I celebrated completing it.

In fact, I wasn't just proud of myself for reaching the finishing line but also for sticking to my workout routine.

On that day, I joined a small percentage of people in the world who completed a marathon. What's more, that day, I proved to myself that I can do anything I want, no matter how big or intimidating the goal might be.

If you have a big goal, just go for it. Don't think about the consequences. If you spend too much time thinking about what you want to do, you'll never accomplish it. Just take that first step.

But do it at a pace you're comfortable with. Create your mental bandwidth budget to know what you can and can't do. Have a set time to worry, and move on once the time is over. When you do what works for you, you can achieve anything.

The Mental Bandwidth Budget

We all have something we can't stop thinking about. It could be a decision you have to make that makes you replay all possible scenarios, or perhaps a conversation you had last weekend that you're convinced went terribly.

It can feel like you're watching a bad movie on repeat. You know exactly what happened in every scene and can even repeat the dialogue, but you're still watching it, over and over. You might even be wondering, *Why am I still thinking about this? Why am I wasting my energy on this? I already don't have energy, and now I'm wasting it like this.*

I'm sure you've been there. You're feeling completely drained and wish you could order an extra dose of energy from a shop. I've been in your shoes. And luckily, I found a solution.

Let me introduce you to the concept of a mental bandwidth budget. It's a way to measure the energy you have, what you need to spend your energy on, and where you can cut.

Just like your financial budget, your mental bandwidth is limited. You only have a certain amount of mental energy, and once it's gone, it's gone. You need to spend it on things that matter most to you and not on the endless loop of overthinking.

Think of your mind as a phone battery. When you use your phone all day to scroll through social media, check work emails, or play mindless games, the battery drains quickly. Before you know it, you need to charge your phone.

Your mind is the same. If you're constantly overthinking things, it can feel like your brain's battery is running on 1%. Unfortunately, unlike your phone, your mind doesn't come with a charger. Sure, sleeping will help you recharge, but we've already discussed how overthinking can affect your sleep.

So, what's the solution? Well, just like you have to pay attention to how you spend your money, you need to manage how you spend your mental energy. Once it's wasted, it's gone.

Take a minute to ask yourself where your mental bandwidth is going. Are you obsessing over that email you sent earlier that didn't get the response you wanted? Maybe you're playing the "what if" game with a decision you made a week ago. Perhaps you're worrying about the future.

The more you focus on these things, the more you end up spinning your wheels, draining your energy, and getting stuck in stress or regret. Instead, ask yourself, "Is this worth my time and energy?"

One of the biggest ways we drain our mental bandwidth is by holding on to the past. This could be a mistake you made at work, a fight you had with a friend, or a past trauma, like being bullied as a child.

Every time you replay that conversation or moment in your mind, you're essentially paying interest on emotional debt. This is the same as paying interest on your car loan. You may not notice how much that takes out of your budget until you do the calculations.

Just like the money you spend on interest could have a better use, the energy you spend on emotional debt could also be spent on something far more useful, like focusing on the present or making better decisions for the future. But, we tend to linger on the past because it's familiar. It's easier to revisit a past failure than to venture into something new and uncertain.

So, how do you stop doing this?

Well, you need to recognize that the past has already happened. No amount of overthinking can change it. Sure, your overthinking about past traumas might have helped you cope with what happened, but is that still the case?

Letting go doesn't mean you're forgetting about something or won't be cautious when faced with a similar situation. It's about freeing up mental space so you can focus on the next step toward a better life.

It's about deciding what you want in the future so you can create your mental bandwidth budget to take you there:

- **Create time to think:** Schedule time during the day for reflection or problem-solving. Maybe it's 15 minutes after lunch to review a conversation or decision. Once this is done, take any actions you can and close the chapter. Don't waste more of your energy thinking about things you can't change.

- **Give yourself permission to let go:** Letting go doesn't mean you don't care about what happened. It means that you're choosing to focus on what you can control today. Take any lessons from that experience, and leave the baggage behind.

- **Prioritize what's important:** Think about the areas of your life that need your attention, such as your health, your relationships, your career, and your personal growth. If need be, revisit the 10-minute exercise to address your difficult thoughts we did in the previous chapter. Allocate your mental bandwidth to these priorities that will improve your life.

- **Create mental reserves:** Just like you save money for the future, you need to save some mental energy for the unexpected. Practice taking mental breaks throughout the day, like going for a quick walk or enjoying a hobby. This will give you more energy for when you need to tackle tougher moments.

Always remember that managing your mental bandwidth isn't about denying yourself the chance to think. It's about being intentional with how you spend that energy.

Create Time to Worry

Now that we've discussed how to save your mental energy by giving yourself limited time to think, let's move on to another thing most of us spend way too much time doing: worrying.

It's like you've got a hundred tabs open in your brain, and no matter how much you try to focus, you can't seem to close any of them. It's exhausting, right?

Here's the thing: Worrying is a part of life. I'm not going to B.S. by telling you to stop worrying altogether. What I will tell you is that you control how much time you spend worrying. You can teach yourself to worry less. You can stop allowing your worries to take over your life.

What if I told you that by setting aside just 10 minutes a day to worry, you'll feel less overwhelmed? Sounds crazy, right? But trust me, this small habit could make a huge difference in how you manage stress and get clarity in your life.

Instead of allowing your worries to pop up randomly and take over, you're giving them a dedicated time slot. You're giving yourself permission to worry. And when the timer goes off, you're done. Now, you give yourself permission to push all that anxiety aside and focus on what's happening in your life.

Let's look at an example: You feel like a good friend is becoming distant. They aren't responding to your messages as quickly as usual, and when they do send you a text, their tone seems off.

You don't know if it's because of something you said or if they're just busy, but it's been bothering you. Every time you think about it, your self-doubt takes over and you question everything you've said to them in the past.

Instead of letting this replay in your mind all day, set a timer for 10 minutes to worry and think it through. Could there be something you can do to reconnect? Maybe you should reach out with a simple "Hey, how's it going?"

Once you've processed it and figured out your next step, stop the worry, take the action, and allow yourself to move on.

Let's look at the easy steps you can follow during your 10-minute worry time:

- **Set a timer:** Find a quiet space. This could be anywhere, even in your car, where you can get some peace and won't be distracted by your phone or the TV. Set a timer for 10 minutes. It's a short enough time that you won't feel like you're wasting the whole day but long enough to let you process worrying thoughts.

- **Focus on what's worrying you:** Think about the things causing you the most stress or anxiety. This could be work-related or personal. Whatever it is, allow yourself to think about it during these 10 minutes.

- **Write it down:** If you're feeling overwhelmed, it can help to make notes of what's on your mind. This might sound simple, but writing about your worries can be helpful. Once it's on paper, it's easier to see what's within your control and what isn't.

- **Look for solutions or let it go:** This is where the magic happens. As you sit there and worry, take a step back and ask yourself: *Is this something I can control or solve right now?* If yes, make a note of the steps you can take. But if it's out of your hands, remind yourself that you don't need to carry that burden all day.

- **Stop worrying after the timer goes off:** The worry session is over. Now, it's time to focus on action instead of overthinking.

10-Minute Exercise: Create Your Log

You'll likely try many different techniques to stop your overthinking. Some will work for you; others won't. Let's now take 10 minutes to create a "what's working" log so you can become more intentional in your actions.

Step 1: Write Down What's Working

Think about areas in your life—personal, professional, or both—where things are starting to move in the right direction. This could be big or small. Here are some examples:

- **Work:** You've been meeting your deadlines, and your boss noticed.

- **Home:** You've been more present with your kids or partner, spending quality time with them in the evenings.

- **Personal growth:** You've been better with your morning routine, getting in 10 minutes of meditation and feeling more grounded.

Write down whatever comes to mind. Celebrate them, even if they're small wins. This list will remind you that you're doing some things right.

Step 2: Write Down What's Not Working

Now, let's talk about the stuff that's still dragging you down. What's holding you back? What are you struggling with? Here are some examples:

- **Work:** Maybe you're stuck on a project that you can't seem to move forward on.

- **Home:** Maybe your work-life balance is off, and you're always thinking about the next big deadline instead of focusing on your family.

- **Personal growth:** Maybe you've been letting your fitness slip. You don't feel like you're progressing or improving.

Again, the goal isn't to beat yourself up here; it's simply to acknowledge what's not working so you can make a plan to fix it.

Step 3: Take Action and Pivot Accordingly

Now comes the fun part: it's time to pivot. Look at what's working and what's not, and then ask yourself questions like: *How can I do more of what's working? What can I let go of to move forward?* Let's break it down:

- **What's working:** What can you do to make sure the project continues to do well? Can you plan more quality time with your family or do something that feeds your energy on a personal level?

- **What's not working:** If you're overwhelmed at work, maybe it's time to delegate more or have a conversation with your boss about shifting responsibilities. If your personal growth is slipping, maybe it's time to schedule your workouts ahead of time so you don't skip them. The goal is to figure out what changes will make the biggest difference.

Step 4: Do It Every Day for a Week

This exercise is not a one-off thing. If you really want to start seeing results, do this for a full week. Each day, take 10 minutes to log what's working and what's not. Then, take action.

Chapter Summary

- Just like you need to manage your finances, you should also manage your mental energy. You only have a limited amount of mental bandwidth.

- Constantly replaying past events, like a bad conversation or a work decision, drains your mental energy and fills your mind with stress and regret. You can't change the past, so focus on the present and future to free up your mental energy.

- Even though worrying is inevitable, you should control how much time you spend on it. Dedicate just 10 minutes each day to worry without letting anxiety take over.

***

There is no magic pill that can take overthinking away. Stopping this cycle takes hard work and dedication. There will be times when you struggle or even relapse, but if you know the signs, are prepared for these challenging times, and treat yourself with compassion, you can make it through without falling back into the trap of overthinking, as we'll discuss in the last chapter.

CHAPTER 8

Training Your Mind to Let Go—For Good

While you were overthinking, you missed everything worth feeling.

–Nitya Prakash

Letting go of something you've been doing for a long time is never easy. I'm sure you've had your own experiences with a habit you're trying to break. In the beginning, it might go well. Then, suddenly, the urge to do it comes back again. Sometimes, with a vengeance.

Let's take smoking as an example. This is a habit that many struggle to break. Some might not have picked up a cigarette in years, only to fall back to their habit, completely out of the blue. It's almost like they press a mental reset button that takes them back.

That is the thing about breaking any habit. For a long time, those pathways in your brain will still be there. Yes, they won't be as strong as they were while you were actively doing this habit, but they will still be lurking in the background. It's almost like a predator, waiting for the right moment to attack.

As much as I want to tell you that once you've been able to go a week or two without overthinking, you'll be cured of this habit. For some people, that might be true. But, for most of us, it just won't be the case.

Most of us will relapse at some point. Unfortunately, this relapse usually happens when we least want it to. When we are under the most stress and anxiety, when we are most vulnerable, our old, bad habits tend to pop out again. You may also stop overthinking in one area of your life but struggle in others.

This is why it's so important to be prepared. When overthinking sticks its ugly head, you need to know what you'll do to stop it in its tracks before it pounces on you. You need to know what you'll do to stay in control of your life and mind.

Perhaps most importantly, you need to treat yourself with compassion. Just because you have a moment (or perhaps a few moments) of overthinking again doesn't mean you're a failure. Don't even think of allowing your mind to take you back there again.

You can do this. You can be prepared for the slip-ups that will happen. You can get back on the proverbial horse to fight your overanalyzing. And you can do this with the kindness you deserve. Because, after all, you're only human.

The Overthinking Relapse Plan

Relapses are part of the process. It's part of being human. No matter what habit you're trying to break, most people will have times when they slip back into old habits.

Backsliding doesn't mean you can't overcome your overthinking. Trust me, I've done it. If I can do it, so can you. It just means that you need to be prepared for your relapses. You need to be ready and know what you're going to do when your mind starts to spiral again. You need to have an overthinking relapse plan.

Having this plan will not only give you peace of mind that you'll be able to stop those mental loops from taking over again. It will also be a map of what you need to do. It will give you an action plan you can immediately start without overthinking how you'll get out of that cycle.

I believe the key to creating your relapse plan is to keep it simple. You don't need to overthink how you'll deal with every single situation in which you may slip up. Instead, you can follow these five steps:

1. **Recognize your triggers:** When you realize you're overthinking, acknowledge it. Tell yourself that you're overthinking. If you can, do this out loud, as your mind responds differently to something you hear than something you think. Catching yourself going back into overthinking is your first win.

2. **Stop your thoughts:** Use an interruption technique to stop your cycle of overthinking. In Chapter 5, we discussed many techniques to help you break your cycle of thoughts and shift your focus.

3. **Reframe the situation:** Change your negative thoughts by focusing on something positive. You can also apply the three-question rule to determine whether your thoughts are based on facts or assumptions or ask yourself if whatever you're overthinking is something you can control.

4. **Choose an action:** Always remember that action ends the paralysis and procrastination that comes with overthinking. No matter how small this action might be, it's a step in the right direction. It's a step that creates movement and momentum.

5. **Choose kindness:** When you're slipping back into overthinking, it's easy to berate yourself. This won't help you move forward. Always treat yourself with compassion, as we'll discuss below.

These five steps might seem simple, but the impact they can have on your ability to break the cycle before it takes hold of your mind can be amazing.

Practice Anti-Overthinking Habits Daily

Breaking a habit like overthinking isn't something you do once and then go on with a life of mental clarity. Having a plan of what you'll do when you slip up is just one way of making sure you leave overthinking in the past.

The other thing you can do to stop overthinking for good is to create habits that will help keep your mind clear. I call these anti-overthinking habits.

Think of these habits as going to a mental gym. If you want to work on your physical strength, you need to lift weights. The same goes for your mental strength. If you want to be resilient and stand strong against your overthinking, you need to practice it regularly.

Here are a few examples of anti-overthinking habits:

- **Practice mindfulness:** Being mindful doesn't only remind you of what's happening in your present; it also calms your mind. You don't have to spend hours being mindful. Even spending 5–10 minutes a day being mindful can make a big difference in becoming more aware of your thoughts and accepting them without judgment. Refer back to Chapter 4 on grounding techniques you can practice during your mindful times.

- **Celebrate small wins:** In the same way small actions can create momentum, celebrating your wins, regardless of how small they may be, creates motivation. If you find yourself deciding without overthinking, pat yourself on the back. Your win might seem small, but you're creating the right mindset to break your cycle of overthinking.

- **Keep things simple:** The more clutter you allow in your life, the more your mind will spiral out of control. Make a habit of keeping things as simple as possible, whether it's your workplace, your home, your schedule, or your goals. This will help to free up your mental bandwidth for the really important things.

The more you practice these basic habits, the stronger you will become mentally, and the easier it will be to recognize when you're overthinking and stop this habit for good.

The Power of Self-Compassion

Take a moment to think about the ideal mindset for overthinking. You're likely thinking about perfectionism, fear of failing, people-pleasing, indecisiveness, or even loss of control.

You're absolutely right. Those are, without a doubt, the big contributors to overthinking. But what do they all have in common?

The answer is simple: self-criticism.

When you're overthinking, you're constantly criticizing yourself for everything you do. You may beat yourself up for saying the wrong thing in a meeting or make yourself believe that you're a complete idiot for making a simple mistake.

The more you criticize yourself, the worse this gets. The worse your anxiety and stress get. So, the cycle continues. Overthinking thrives on self-criticism. It's as simple as that.

How can you break free from this? While all the techniques we discussed in this book will help you reframe these negative thoughts, I want to leave you with a last one: self-compassion.

It's about being kind to yourself. It's about not judging yourself as harshly when you make a mistake or say the wrong thing. It's about realizing that you're only a human who is just trying your best.

Self-compassion ties in with the third question in the three-question rule we discussed in Chapter 2: Is it kind? Would you say that to a friend? Or would you help the friend to see the positives, no matter how bleak the situation may seem?

Let's say you're in a brainstorming meeting at work. You suddenly get an idea, and without thinking it through, you share it with your colleagues. Unfortunately, it wasn't received well, with a coworker immediately pointing out flaws in your plan that you never considered.

A typical overthinker would now drain their mental bandwidth with thoughts about how incompetent they might have looked or what their colleagues will now be thinking of them. But by practicing compassion, you're changing this narrative.

Now, you're telling yourself something like, *That didn't exactly go according to plan. But, at least I tried to contribute. I showed my colleagues that I'm part of the team. What can I do better next time?*

This change not only helped you to stop the otherwise endless cycle of self-criticism, but you're immediately thinking of the next step. You're immediately looking at how you can create momentum to take you forward.

Self-compassion is about understanding that you will make mistakes but that you should forgive yourself for them instead of allowing your mind to spiral with criticism.

You don't need to always have everything figured out. You don't need to regret past mistakes. You can learn from them. You can be the best version of yourself, and that's always good enough.

10-Minute Exercise: The Mental Reset Check-In

This last exercise is one that I encourage you to do every week, perhaps on a Sunday. This can become one of your anti-overthinking habits and will take only 10 minutes per week. It's all about taking time to reflect on the week that has passed and prepare you for the week that lies ahead. Here's how to do it:

- **Relax in a quiet space:** Find a place where you won't be interrupted. This can even be in the car parked at the grocery store. Relax with a few deep breathing exercises.

- **Think about what went well:** Start this exercise by focusing on the positives of the past week. What did you do well at work? Maybe you finished a difficult project or closed a big deal. Perhaps the positive of your work week was just treating colleagues with kindness. Similarly, what went well in your personal life? Did you stick to your workout routine? Were you able to spend more time with loved ones? Perhaps you finally got to read that book collecting dust on the shelf.

- **Consider what you can improve on:** I choose not to call this the "what went wrong," as this creates even more negativity and room for self-criticism. Identifying things to improve on gives this a positive, compassionate spin. It's about getting better, not beating yourself up.

- **Create an action plan:** Take one or two things from your previous list and decide on an action you can take to improve. Keep this small and simple so it doesn't overwhelm you. This can be something like scheduling 15 minutes in the morning to create a to-do list for the day or doing one device-free night in the week to spend time with your loved ones.

- **Close with a positive:** End your mental check-in with a quick positive affirmation. This can be as simple as "I'm doing the best I can, and that's good enough," or "Every day is an opportunity to be better." If you can, say it out loud.

Chapter Summary

- Whenever you work on breaking habits like overthinking, you'll likely experience relapses. You can prepare for them by creating an overthinking relapse plan.

- It's best to keep this plan as simple as you can. Steps to include are recognizing triggers, stopping thoughts with interruption techniques, reframing negative thoughts, choosing an action, and practicing self-kindness.

- Develop anti-overthinking habits, such as practicing mindfulness, celebrating small wins, and keeping life simple to reduce slip-ups.

- Overthinking is fueled by self-criticism, which increases anxiety and stress. Practicing self-compassion can help to break this cycle.

***

You're ready to make your overthinking a thing of the past. You're ready to break the cycle of constant mental loops. You're ready to reclaim your life. Now, I want to challenge you: Try to go the next 21 days without overthinking, as we'll discuss next.

CONCLUSION

Your Life Beyond Overthinking

The best things happen when you're not overthinking it.

–Ben Zobrist

Take a few minutes to think back to a time when overthinking ruled your mind. A time when your thoughts would spiral out of control, leaving you feeling defeated and like a failure. A time when you couldn't make even the simplest decisions without second-guessing yourself.

It's tough, hey? It's tough to recognize what you put yourself through, day in and day out. It's tough to realize how much time you've wasted.

But it's in the past. It's no longer part of your life. You've come a long way. You're allowed to be very proud of yourself.

Yes, there will be days when you fall back into old habits. You may take too long to make a decision. You may worry again about how something you've said might have been interpreted. But with your relapse plan handy, you won't allow these negative thoughts to take control of your life again.

155

You now have the right mindset to end your thoughts before they spiral. You understand your triggers to your overthinking and know how to identify repeating thought patterns. You've become more mindful in your daily life. You've made micro-actions part of your routine. And you know how you want to spend your mental bandwidth.

You know that the goal isn't to reach perfection. It's about the progress you make. The more you work on overcoming your habit of overthinking, the easier it will get. Because overthinking is only a habit. It's not part of you. It's something that you've learned to do. And it's something you're now learning not to do anymore.

Now, I want to leave you with one final 21-day challenge. I'm sure you've heard people say it takes 21 days to break a habit. Three weeks of commitment, that's all I'm asking. Your reward? A lifetime of no overthinking.

I don't know about you, but that sounds like a good deal to me.

The bonus here is that it won't take up much of your time. All you need to do is pay close attention to your thoughts. Whenever you catch your mind spiraling for more than five minutes, you do a quick mental reset. This basically means you use a technique, such as telling yourself, out loud if you can, something like, "I've been thinking about this for too long now. I'm done now. I'm moving on."

This helps to clear your mind, refocus on what you're busy with, and give you a sense of control when you're feeling overwhelmed, stressed, or stuck. It's like pressing the reset button on your mental state. When you do a mental reset, you essentially start fresh, beginning the 21-day challenge all over again.

You can also use a tangible item to help you with this. Every time you start overthinking too much, switch a ring to another finger, pinch yourself, or snap your wrist with a rubber band you wear as a bracelet. Then, do your mental reset and restart the 21-day challenge.

It might sound silly, I know. I also had my doubts when I heard about this for the first time. But it makes you more aware of your overthinking, which, in turn, reduces this habit.

Make a note every time you do a mental reset. Quickly jot down what you were thinking about, and move on. This isn't to give you something to overthink about later. Sure, you can use it to identify patterns of overthinking, but the main purpose here is to measure your progress. It will help to motivate you as you restart the challenge.

There is no greater feeling than seeing how the number of mental resets you need daily declines.

If you struggle to let go of these thoughts, do a 10-minute worry time. Set your timer. Allow yourself those minutes to worry about what's bothering you. Why waste your mental energy on it if it's not in your control? If you can change it, decide on an action you can take to move forward. And, once the timer goes off, let it go.

Treat yourself with kindness if you have a day where your mental resets have increased. You're doing a fantastic job. Breaking a habit like overthinking is difficult, but the more you do it, the longer you'll go without overthinking. The rewards are greater than any frustration you may experience.

Simply acknowledge that you've had a difficult day, reset, and move on.

Never forget how far you've come. Never forget how you used to struggle with overthinking. Here is the key: Never again allow this into your life. Your past is just that—your past. It doesn't have to be part of your future. Use the memories of your struggles to push you toward the life you want.

You have the knowledge, skills, and techniques to end your overthinking for good. Take 10 minutes daily for micro-actions to keep the momentum going. Create your relapse plan. Trust yourself, and take it one step at a time to live the life you deserve.

A Thank You Note From Me to You

Thank you so much for reading this book. With so many book options out there, I'm grateful you chose this one and stuck with it until the end.

I hope something in these pages sparked a shift, gave you clarity, or encouraged you to stop overthinking for good.

If this book made an impact on you, I'd be so thankful if you left a quick review. Just search for the book title—**"How to Stop Overthinking for Good:** The No B.S. Solution to Worry Less, Beat Procrastination, and Reclaim Your Time in Only 10 Minutes a Day"— on the platform where you purchased it and leave your honest thoughts.

Your feedback helps more people discover the message—and it gives me the encouragement to keep creating meaningful content.

Your support means the world.

With gratitude,

Shelomo

Let's Stay Connected

If you're interested in more of my books, head over to:

www.labelstolegacy.com/books

For speaking engagements, podcast appearances, business opportunities, or to just say hello, you can reach me directly at: **shelomo@labelstolegacy.com**

Thanks again for being part of this journey. Let's keep growing together.

References

Angelou, M. (n.d.). *A quote by Maya Angelou*. GoodReads. https://www.goodreads.com/quotes/228308-you-may-not-control-all-the-events-that-happen-to

Arnold, P. (2021, May 5). *A quote in "40+ best overthinking quotes to calm your mind."* Crazy Laura Quotes. https://www.crazylauraquotes.com/overthinking-quotes/

Bauwens, C. (2021, April 14). *3 quick questions to ask to stop overthinking*. Coach Carlene. https://coachcarlene.com/3-quick-questions-to-stop-overthinking/

Bonaparte, N. (2021, May 5). *A quote in "40+ best overthinking quotes to calm your mind."* Crazy Laura Quotes. https://www.crazylauraquotes.com/overthinking-quotes/

Bowling, V. (2021, November 24). *9 simple habits to stop overthinking and start living in the now*. Bit of Self-Care. https://www.bitofselfcare.com/post/9-simple-habits-to-stop-overthinking

Camacho, B. (2024, February 28). *Why do I overthink everything? A psychiatrist explains.* Talkiatry. https://www.talkiatry.com/blog/why-do-i-overthink-everything

Chand, S. P., & Marwaha, R. (2023, April 24). *Anxiety.* National Library of Medicine; StatPearls Publishing. https://www.ncbi.nlm.nih.gov/books/NBK470361/

Clear, J. (2018). *Habits guide: How to build good habits and break bad ones.* James Clear. https://jamesclear.com/habits

Dankaert, E. (2025, March 4). *Overthinking: How to release your perfectionism handbrake.* Dr E. https://esmarildadankaert.com/2025/03/04/overthinking-how-to-release-your-perfectionism-handbrake/

Duhigg, C. (2014). *Power of Habit: Why We Do What We Do in Life and Business.* Random House Trade Paperbacks. (Original work published 2012)

Fletcher, A. (2024, April 2). *How to navigate overthinking with compassionate awareness.* Mindful. https://www.mindful.org/how-to-navigate-overthinking-with-compassionate-awareness/

Frederick, R. (2019, October 30). *Why your brain is on the lookout for danger.* Center for Courageous Living. https://www.cfcliving.com/brain-threat-detector/

Gardener, A. (2024, August 27). *How stress affects the brain.* American Brain Foundation. https://www.americanbrainfoundation.org/how-stress-affects-the-brain/

Green, J. (n.d.). *A quote from John Green.* GoodReads. https://www.goodreads.com/quotes/8848435-there-is-hope-even-when-your-brain-tells-you-there

How overthinking becomes a problem. (2024, November 8). TalktoAngel. https://www.talktoangel.com/blog/how-overthinking-becomes-a-problem

How to break the negative thinking loop. (n.d.). MensLine Australia. https://mensline.org.au/signs-and-symptoms-of-depression/how-to-break-the-negative-thinking-loop/

Illinois Recovery Center. (2024, July 13). *Is overthinking a trauma response?* Illinois Recovery Center. https://illinoisrecoverycenter.com/is-overthinking-a-trauma-response/

Jennings, K.-A., & Kubala, J. (2023, July 12). *16 simple ways to relieve stress and anxiety.* Healthline. https://www.healthline.com/nutrition/16-ways-relieve-stress-anxiety

Kaiser, B. N., Haroz, E. E., Kohrt, B. A., Bolton, P. A., Bass, J. K., & Hinton, D. E. (2015). "Thinking too much": A systematic review of a common idiom of distress. *Social Science & Medicine, 147*, 170–183. https://doi.org/10.1016/j.socscimed.2015.10.044

King, M. L. (2021, May 5). *A quote in "40+ best overthinking quotes to calm your mind."* Crazy Laura Quotes. https://www.crazylauraquotes.com/overthinking-quotes/

Krockow, E. M. (2023, August 31). *The dangers of overthinking.* Psychology Today. https://www.psychologytoday.com/blog/stretching-theory/202308/the-dangers-of-overthinking

LeWine, H. E. (2024, April 3). *Understanding the stress response.* Harvard Health. https://www.health.harvard.edu/staying-healthy/understanding-the-stress-response

McAdam, E. (2022, September 1). *Overthinking 4: Social anxiety: "Why did I say that?!"* Therapy in a Nutshell. https://therapyinanutshell.com/overthinking-4-social-anxiety-why-did-i-say-that/

Mind. (2022, March). *Causes of stress.* Mind. https://www.mind.org.uk/information-support/types-of-mental-health-problems/stress/causes-of-stress/

Morin, A. (2024, June 18). *How to stop overthinking*. Verywell Mind. https://www.verywellmind.com/how-to-know-when-youre-overthinking-5077069

National Institute of Mental Health. (2022). *Generalized anxiety disorder: When worry gets out of control.* National Institute of Mental Health. https://www.nimh.nih.gov/health/publications/generalized-anxiety-disorder-gad

National Institute of Mental Health. (2024). *Post-traumatic stress disorder.* National Institute of Mental Health. https://www.nimh.nih.gov/health/topics/post-traumatic-stress-disorder-ptsd

Perry, E. (2024, January 14). *What is habit stacking? 5 examples.* BetterUp. https://www.betterup.com/blog/habit-stacking

Prakash, N. (2021, May 5). *A quote in "40+ best overthinking quotes to calm your mind."* Crazy Laura Quotes. https://www.crazylauraquotes.com/overthinking-quotes/

Robinson, J. (2024a, May 6). *How does the brain think?* The Conversation. https://theconversation.com/how-does-the-brain-think-224228

Robinson, J. (2024b, November 22). *How worrying affects your body.* WebMD. https://www.webmd.com/balance/how-worrying-affects-your-body

rstambridge. (2023, July 14). *How to stop overthinking social interactions by a therapist.* Contented Mind - Therapy & Mindfulness. https://contentedmind.uk/how-to-stop-overthinking-social-interactions-by-self-esteem-therapist/

Salmansohn, K. (2021, May 5). *A quote in "40+ best overthinking quotes to calm your mind."* Crazy Laura Quotes. https://www.crazylauraquotes.com/overthinking-quotes/

Scott, S. J. (2014). *Habit stacking: 97 small life changes that take five minutes or less.* Archangel Ink.

Shaw, G. B. (2021, May 5). *A quote in "40+ best overthinking quotes to calm your mind."* Crazy Laura Quotes. https://www.crazylauraquotes.com/overthinking-quotes/

Sims, K. (n.d.). *Overthinking and self-esteem.* Birch Psychology. https://www.birchpsychology.com/birchs-blog/2023/8/6/overthinking-and-self-esteem

Smith, S. (2018, October 4). *5-4-3-2-1 coping technique for anxiety.* University of Rochester Medical Center.

https://www.urmc.rochester.edu/behavioral-health-partners/bhp-blog/april-2018/5-4-3-2-1-coping-technique-for-anxiety

Tanasugarn, A. (2024, April 10). *4 trauma responses that may be hurting your relationships.* Psychology Today. https://www.psychologytoday.com/us/blog/understanding-ptsd/202404/4-trauma-responses-that-may-be-hurting-your-relationships

Wilding, M. (2022, June 7). How to tell the difference between fear and intuition. *Forbes.* https://www.forbes.com/sites/melodywilding/2022/06/07/how-to-tell-the-difference-between-fear-and-intuition/

Williams, J. M. (2023, March 13). *How to stop overthinking and take action.* Medium. https://drjae.medium.com/free-yourself-from-paralysis-by-analysis-how-to-stop-overthinking-take-action-4-42ec4c51488

Wright, P. (2024, January 5). *The effect of stress on the brain and ways to manage it.* Nuvance Health. https://www.nuvancehealth.org/health-tips-and-news/the-effect-of-stress-on-the-brain-and-ways-to-manage-it

Zobrist, B. (2021, May 5). *A quote in "40+ best overthinking quotes to calm your mind."* Crazy Laura Quotes. https://www.crazylauraquotes.com/overthinking-quotes/